WHAT KEY LEADERS HAVE TO SAY:

Dear Students, I hope you take great pride in all your hard work and accomplishments. America needs students like you who are working hard in school, dreaming big dreams, and improving our communities. Our country faces great challenges, but we will overcome them if we join together in common purpose. I encourage you to continue to put your best effort into everything you do, and please know I expect great things from you. Young people like you—the future leaders of our nation—inspire me and give me great hope for the future. Michelle and I wish you all the best.

—BARACK OBAMA
44th President of the United States

To the Valley Christian High ISS Team, with best wishes.

—GEORGE W. BUSH
43rd President of the United States

For a quarter of a century your institution has provided its students with the best—not only the best academic content but the best values as well. By recognizing the importance of the Judeo-Christian values in education, you offer your students a treasure that both trains the mind and fills the heart with hope. Nancy and I congratulate you and wish you every success in your efforts. God bless you.

—RONALD REAGAN
40th President of the United States

To Valley Christian, Great work on your ISS experiments!

—BUZZ ALDRIN
Apollo XI Astronaut (2nd man to walk on the moon)

Aim high in all you do!

—TOM JONES
NASA Astronaut (completed four space shuttle flights)

Dear Students, I understand that you and your fellow students from Valley Christian High School recently became the first high school students in the nation to have an experiment aboard the International Space Station. I applaud your hard work. I know you and your teams have earned this honor through much dedication and perseverance. . . . By sending the first student-designed experiment into space, you will be sure to inspire future generations to come.

—**BARBARA BOXER**
Former U.S. Senator

To the ISS and Satellite Development Teams of Valley Christian High School, with congratulations.

—**JOHN GLENN**
NASA Astronaut, Former U.S. Senator

To the ISS Team of Valley Christian High School: Your pursuit of knowledge in the confines of your experiment that will soon fly into the glorious free fall of space is a sign of hope for us all. You are not merely asking questions of nature, you are seeking answers—of the two, the much more difficult and provocative activity. . . . Bravo and God speed. You are gifted, each of you, and I exhort you.

—**TOM HANKS**
Actor

I am proud to join the U.S. Department of Education in honoring you as the first private high school in California to receive the prestigious Blue Ribbon Award—a designation reflecting the achievement of your students in the top 10 percent of all high school students in the nation. This national recognition is a worthy tribute to your dedicated pursuit of excellence. I also commend each Valley Christian student for your commitment to working hard and realizing your goals.

—**ARNOLD SCHWARZENEGGER**
Former Governor of California

CLIFFORD E. DAUGHERTY
AND DANNY D. KIM

WITH JIM NELSON BLACK

QUEST
~FOR~
QUALITY
EDUCATION

THE SKY IS NOT THE LIMIT!

QUEST *for* EXCELLENCE | MEDIA

Quest for Quality Education
(SECOND EDITION)

Library of Congress Cataloging-in-Publication Data

Daugherty, Clifford E.
    Quest for quality education: the sky is not the limit / Clifford E. Daugherty, Ed.D., and Danny D. Kim
p. cm.

ISBN: 978-1-7341216-3-6
ISBN: 978-0-9964207-9-2 (eBook)

Printed in the United States of America
20 21 22 23 24 25 26 27   (LBM)   10 9 8 7 6 5 4 3 2

Manuscript Prepared by Jim Nelson Black, Ph.D. | www.jnblack.com

Design by Peter Gloege | LOOK Design Studio

DEDICATION

TABLE OF CONTENTS

"FROM THEIR HILLTOP CAMPUS

OVERLOOKING SILICON VALLEY,

THIS CHRISTIAN SCHOOL

IS HELPING TO RENEW A PASSION

FOR LEARNING IN

AMERICA'S PUBLIC SCHOOLS."

— DR. ED SILVOSO

TRANSFORM
OURWORLD

CHAPTER 1

THE VISION:
A BIRD'S-EYE VIEW

VALLEY CHRISTIAN SCHOOLS is not only one of the most successful schools on the American West Coast, but it's also a model of what can be accomplished in both public and private schools everywhere when a passion for excellence and resolute faith come together. The fifty-seven-acre campus at the summit of Skyway Drive overlooks the city of San Jose and the sprawling landscape of Silicon Valley. With more than 2,750 students in kindergarten through twelfth grades, VCS is often named one of the best private schools in the nation.

The school's $200 million educational campuses offer some of the most advanced educational opportunities anywhere, including comprehensive elementary, junior high, and high school programs. Founded on the school's QUEST for Excellence™ and Excellence Brings Influence® strategies, initiatives include Academic Achievement, Artistic Beauty, and Athletic Distinction™ (A³ ™).

With support from leading technology giants, an amazing faculty, and a team of extraordinary mentors, students benefit from the school's Applied Math, Science, and Engineering (AMSE) Institute.

Valley's students have enabled others from schools around the world to place hundreds of research projects aboard the International Space Station (ISS) through the school's Quest for Space program, headed by my colleague and co-author, Danny Kim. Teams of students in the school's Quest for Oceans program are launching a revolutionary new concept for student research on the ocean floor. Thanks to the skill and expertise demonstrated by these students, Valley's underwater researchers now have a science experiment lab attached to the deep-sea platform of the Monterey Bay Aquarium Research Institute (MBARI). Other AMSE programs such as aeronautics, hydroponics, an observatory, robotics, and rocketry are among the ever-growing opportunities for students.

The U.S. Department of Education awarded the No Child Left Behind Blue Ribbon recognition to all three schools (elementary, junior high, and high school) for superior academic performance. The junior high earned the Intel School of Distinction honor for demonstrating excellence in math education through innovative teaching and learning environments, as well as the coveted Intel STAR Innovator Award. The high school math team has won multiple first-place awards in the annual statewide math competition.

At the same time, the VCS Conservatory of the Arts draws international recognition, with award-winning programs in art, choir, dance, filmmaking, graphic arts, jazz band, journalism, theater, a full symphony orchestra, and more. A few of the many Conservatory of the Arts achievements include:

✧ Marching in the Tournament of Roses Parade

✧ Recognition by *Downbeat* magazine as the top high school jazz ensemble in the nation on multiple occasions

✧ Winning multiple First Place Gold Medals at the
Winter Guard International World Championship
Finals by Valley Christian High School's (VCHS's) Per-
forming Indoor Ensemble (multimedia band)

✧ Designation as one of the top theater programs in the
nation by *Stage Directions* magazine

✧ National championships in both the ensemble and solo
categories at the national Contest of Champions by
Vivid, VCHS's conservatory dance team

✧ Recognition at national and international piano competitions, including the National Young Arts Competition, U.S. Open Music Competition, and the Aarhus
International Piano Competition

Athletic programs are highly ranked in the state, year after year.
Our motto, "Pursuing victory with honor," and teaching life lessons
through disciplined training and true competition embody the philosophy of "Athletic Distinction." Distinctive achievements include:

✧ Fielding forty-eight high school competitive teams in
20 different sports

✧ Recognition as the number one ranked varsity baseball
team in the nation by MaxPreps computer rankings, as
of this writing

✧ Designation as the California State Athletic School of
the Year by Cal-Hi Sports

Among its impressive athletic facilities, the beyond-Olympic-
sized swimming pool on Skyway campus at the top of the hill is one of
the largest in Northern California. Even more notably, Valley athletes

enjoy status among those most eagerly recruited by the nation's prestigious university athletic programs.

Equally impressive are the outreach programs led by hundreds of Valley's student volunteers who mentor children in the local public schools in academics, the arts, and athletics. Junior University and the Lighthouse Initiative™ (JULI™), developed in concert with public schools in the South Bay Area, radiate a much-needed infusion of hope and encouragement. They make the Quest for Quality Education a reality for students in the neighborhood public schools. Together, these programs offer a practical model for transforming the culture of schools in communities all over America.

These examples are just a small sampling of what's happening at Valley Christian Schools. We recite this list of achievements not to boast about what our students and faculty accomplish, but rather our purpose is to illustrate the dramatic contrast between past challenges and the extraordinary gains the school has made since we dedicated ourselves unreservedly to the QUEST for Excellence.

A MONUMENTAL CHALLENGE

Our journey—from the depressing and poorly equipped campus I encountered on my first day on the job to today's modern, state-of-the-art college preparatory school—didn't happen overnight. We had many hardships to overcome and many lessons to learn, but God prepared the ground before us and opened doors in miraculous ways. Along the journey, He opened our eyes to opportunities we could hardly have imagined in those early years.

The story of Valley Christian Schools begins back in 1956. During a home Bible study, Dave and Edie Wallace started praying about starting a school that would provide a nurturing environment and a strong foundation of Christian values for children in the South Bay Area. They believed parents are the primary educators of their children, so they wanted the school to operate as a partnership between parents and teachers, equipping students academically and socially while providing a strong religious foundation. The goal was to prepare young people to become leaders in their communities and the world, and that aim has remained at the heart of our educational philosophy ever since. But keeping the schools afloat would prove to be a monumental challenge.

From its opening in 1960 until around 1983, Valley grew into one of the largest Christian school systems in the country, with 1,400 students on five campuses. By 1986, however, the school had fallen on hard times with leadership problems and serious financial concerns. The staff faced a long list of challenges, including the impending loss of the high school's lease in June of 1987 and internal conflicts about the overall mission and vision of the school.

When a friend approached me and asked if I would consider taking the head of school position as superintendent, I was reluctant. I had been a teacher and school administrator, and most recently served as a successful financial planning representative. Yet, through a series of extraordinary events, I received and accepted the job offer, and started work in July 1986.

My first sight of the high school distressed me. It occupied an abandoned public school campus in the Cambrian community of San Jose. Trash and debris covered the grounds. Weeds taller than the six-foot cyclone fence encircling the thirty-acre grounds made the place look deserted. The school couldn't afford adequate landscaping or maintenance, so the overall appearance was depressing. Anyone could see the magnitude of the challenge. The chances of turning things around didn't appear good, and VCS was drowning in red ink. But that wasn't the worst of it.

The school's academic standards were inconsistent at best. I remember asking a teacher why she had given a "B" for an essay filled with syntax, spelling, and grammar errors. The reply startled me: "This is history, not an English course. We grade on content, not composition." In another situation, the journalism instructor chased students around the classroom. "Just having fun," he said. His behavior resulted in the loss of employment after our efforts to remedy his attitude and behavior failed to produce change.

Some generous soul donated a lab full of scientific computers. Sadly, no one knew the computer language, including the teacher. The students came to class faithfully every day without ever touching the computers. There's no telling what they learned, but to hold their interest, the teacher allowed them to sneak off campus to buy snacks from the local donut shop.

The faculty and staff received salaries less than half the compensation for teachers in the local public schools. Because VCS principals fought a losing battle trying to attract quality teachers with low wages, academic standards took a precipitous decline. The future home of the high school remained in doubt, so teachers and parents found it virtually impossible to make long-range plans with that kind of uncertainty.

To make matters worse, I discovered there were disproportionately serious problems with alcohol and tobacco on campus, teen pregnancies, and interpersonal conflicts affecting both students and faculty. Thanks to all the confusion and uncertainty, enrollment shrank to fewer than a thousand students, and from five to three campuses.

After many months wondering whether our high school students would have a home in the fall, we were finally able to negotiate a one-year lease extension in April 1987, giving us a little breathing room. Then, in May, the high school principal resigned, and I took on the additional role as principal while continuing as superintendent.

As we wrestled with all these problems, including the school's mounting debt, the atmosphere pervading the high school campus troubled me. The administration had adopted explicit rules for dress, behavior, and lifestyle in an effort to "keep the high school Christian." Although the aim was to maintain moral behavior, the overly strict regulations blurred the distinction between biblical principles and institutional standards.

Boys had to keep their hair short, and girls couldn't wear pants. Cheerleaders weren't permitted to combine movement and music lest they cross the line into "sinful" dance. All forms of affection between boys and girls, including hand-holding, met with immediate disapproval. And the school band was not allowed to play "Rock Around the Clock," because "rock music" was strictly forbidden.

The standards and their harsh enforcement irritated students and their families to the point that some began referring to the school as "Valley Christian Prison." At the same time, some parents of local public school students threatened to send their children to Valley if they got out of line. One VCS parent warned his son, "If attending Valley doesn't improve your behavior, I'll transfer you to a military boarding school."

Time for a Change

It was obvious: The legalistic approach to school discipline was a disaster. When students disagreed with the school's standards, they often thought they were rejecting God and His standards as well. The tension and distrust between students, their parents, and the faculty persisted. This toxic atmosphere no doubt contributed to the enrollment decline and the struggle to hire good teachers.

With the support of the board of directors, the Student/Parent Handbook was rewritten to make a clear distinction between school rules and authentic biblical Christian principles. The regulation on boys' haircuts was relaxed. Pants became an acceptable part of the dress code for girls. The rule against any "public display of affection" became a rule against inappropriate displays of affection. These and other changes showed up all over campus. Cheerleaders added music to their routines, while parents, not the school, decided whether private parties would include dancing. And the band played "Rock Around the Clock." The new approach helped foster a much more congenial atmosphere and attracted rather than coerced students toward respectful behavior.

With the understanding that doubt often precedes mature faith, we began to encourage more discussion, debate, and analysis regarding matters of faith. Students were challenged to think about what they believe and why, and thoughtfully consider the teachings of Jesus before committing to following Him as their Lord and Savior. With this approach, we no longer required students to express their Christian faith as a requirement for admission. Eventually, they came to believe it was a privilege to attend Valley Christian High School.

THE QUEST FOR EXCELLENCE

When I proposed "QUEST for Excellence" as the school theme in 1991, I thought it was a catchy phrase that might help inspire higher levels of performance. I hoped it might send a message that the students, faculty, and staff at Valley Christian Schools were determined to pursue quality in all we do. At first, I wondered if the theme would resonate with our constituents, but the power of the QUEST for Excellence caught me off guard. Its potency not only inspired our people; it seemed to have a life of its own.

The courage to dream impossible dreams, to discover the unknown, and to predict seemingly impossible success as though it could not fail was exhilarating. It was like winning a championship or finding a treasure we never knew existed. I now believe the quest concept was a divine infusion of God's creative works, an example of what we have come to call "divine downloads."

The QUEST for Excellence became the foundation for the amazing development of Valley Christian Schools. Eventually, through a remarkable sequence of events, I came to see that the power of the quest reaches beyond our faith-based communities to touch and transform our wider communities, including our public schools.

Within the QUEST for Excellence is a passion for truth and what we now call Common Virtues™, based on the "self-evident truths" described in the United States Declaration of Independence.

"All men are created equal," it says. "Life, liberty, and the pursuit of happiness" are among the "unalienable rights" granted to all people by "their Creator." Out of such truths flow virtues such as mutual respect, the dignity of every person, kindness, honesty, integrity, and treating others the way you would want them to treat you. As time went on, these ideas would take on much greater significance for us. They had the power to give birth to America, and they have the power to transform America's public schools. Such a transformation would bring the United States once again to rank among the world's leading educational systems.

During the development of VCS, I often wondered why the QUEST for Excellence theme produced such powerful results. We had implemented new programs dedicated to "Academic Achievement, Artistic Beauty, and Athletic Distinction," which we now refer to as "A to the third power" or A^3 to reflect the exponential impact of a comprehensive education. Our students enjoy magnificent facilities, and the schools have a well-deserved reputation for excellence. We receive many more applications for admission than we can accept.

But why? To some observers, it seemed as though VCS had some sort of unfair advantage. One day during an administrative conference, a respected Christian educator said to me, "You just happened to be in the right place at the right time." The comment caught me off guard. I thought, *Can that be right? Maybe there was a grain of truth in what he said.* We resided in Silicon Valley, and our student body included the children of dot-com pioneers and philanthropists who helped in various ways, including large capital gifts. That much was true, but I believed those factors were far from the real explanation. The educator's perspective seemed to imply that mere chance, not divine Providence, was the reason for Valley's success. I knew that was not the case.

The QUEST for Excellence is a model all schools, individuals, businesses, and professions can emulate. I came to see that similar kinds of success can be replicated anywhere if the motivation and dedication are the same. If being in the right place at the right time were the school's only advantage, any unforeseen disruption could have brought our plans to a screeching halt. If, however, Valley Christian Schools had been built and sustained by universal and divinely ordained principles involving the QUEST for Excellence and a commitment to quality education, the VCS model could be repeated many times over.

The success of VCS cannot be merely a matter of being in the right place at the right time. We've discovered the QUEST for Excellence principles working in many other places, including areas without the advantages of Silicon Valley. Any place at any time can be the right place and time, because, as our Declaration makes clear, we can rely on "divine Providence" as the means to "life, liberty, and the pursuit of happiness." These great blessings, which we at Valley and other educators in our neighborhood describe as "goodness, peace, and joy," are available everywhere.

Recognizing where it all began, and remembering the hardships we've had to overcome, I know beyond a doubt that God built and sustains Valley Christian Schools. I try to tell school administrators and marketplace professionals everywhere I go that God can be counted on to do the same in their communities, businesses, and personal lives. When guests visit our campus and tell me what a great job I've done building VCS, I am quick to say how thankful I am to serve at Valley Christian Schools while God is doing His great works. And He is able and willing to do similar "excellent works" through you, the educators, and students in your community schools.

A BIGGER AND BOLDER VISION

Three critical principles lie at the core of Valley Christian Schools' success. They serve as the fuel for both the QUEST for Excellence and now the Quest for Quality Education, the focus of this book.

The first principle is the belief that true excellence reflects the nature, character, and works of God. This premise challenges every student, teacher, parent, and administrator in the VCS community to strive for the highest standards. Our theme verse says, "Whatever you do, do it heartily, as to the Lord."[2]

The second principle is the belief that Excellence Brings Influence. Why should Christians pursue excellence with a passion? Because excellence brings influence, and we are compelled by our beliefs to serve as instruments of God's love to all people, using our influence to extend goodness, peace, and joy to our communities and the world.

The third principle is what I call "access to the omnis." Every "divine download" and miraculous event in this book is connected to this principle. Scripture teaches that God is omnipotent, that is, all-powerful. He is also omnipresent, meaning He is everywhere at all times. And God is omniscient, meaning He is all-knowing. His very nature qualifies Him as the only ultimate, all-powerful, everywhere-present, and all-knowing God of the universe. Access to the omnis, then, describes how God makes His resources available to those who seek to serve as conduits of His great works to accomplish His loving purposes.[3]

Hundreds of headmasters, principals, and school board members have come to visit Valley Christian Schools over the years with questions about building excellent Christian schools in their communities. I wondered if I could say with confidence that God is willing and able to do the same miraculous works for schools in other communities. Could other Christian educators expect the same sorts of miracles we've experienced, or was the development of our school a unique phenomenon? I never doubted that God could build a great school anywhere He pleases, but I wondered if it might be a bit presumptuous to say God is *willing* to build a great school system in any community.

As I reflected on the approximately $62 million annual budget it would take to administer another school our size in today's economy, I doubted whether enough resources could be available to build such great schools everywhere. Given my doubts, I decided to take the Apostle James' advice: "If any of you lacks wisdom, let him ask of God, who gives to all liberally."[4] So I looked back at some of the biblical passages I often relied on in situations like this, and I asked God for an answer to my question.

At the time, I had a default perspective that only Christian schools could foster godly character because of the U.S. Supreme Court rulings of the 1960s. So I thought building Christian schools in every community seemed like the only option. But I was in for a big surprise. The paradigm shift began for me when I reflected on the Declaration of Independence. Then I understood how calling on the legacy of America's founding principles could restore goodness, peace, and joy to all children in all schools, including public schools, regardless of their religious or socioeconomic circumstances.

Eventually, as I relate in more detail in the following chapters, we decided to lend a helping hand to students in many schools. Hellyer Elementary, a public school here in San Jose, and Grace Public School in the slums of Delhi, India, stand out as great examples. These were schools in distressed academic and socioeconomic circumstances: underfunded, with strained facilities, struggling to educate students from some of the poorest families in their respective areas. When these schools needed help, we took on the challenge, and we were not disappointed.

The Quest for Quality Education extends the concepts of the QUEST for Excellence by encouraging and enabling Christians and people of good will to build bridges of opportunity to all children in our public, private, charter, and home schools. Mentors and volunteers, working in cooperation with teachers, can have a tremendous influence on our nation's future when they invest in the next generation. This educational transformation can occur even in communities without schools like VCS to partner with their local schools. Individuals and small groups can get involved directly by offering their time, talents, and expertise to their neighborhood schools. Indeed, this involvement of community members plays a crucial role in bringing resources that might not otherwise be available to public schools with limited budgets.

Also, those willing to pray for their neighborhood schools can have a strategic impact by clearing the way for goodness, peace, and joy to flow to places in great need of these blessings.

You will hear more about these stories, but the lesson for us is clear: The QUEST for Excellence, which is the starting point for the Quest for Quality Education, is within reach of every school and every child, regardless of where they happen to live.

In other countries, pursuing this quest might be a matter of perseverance, trusting God to provide the right opportunity and the right moment. In America, the Constitution of the United States guarantees certain rights. The free exercise clause of the First Amendment assures Americans that religious liberty is the right of every citizen. With that knowledge and this understanding awakened in me, I now look back on the hesitation I had felt when I was inclined to turn and walk away from the problems at Valley Christian Schools, and I wonder, *What if I had walked away? What if I had refused God's call on my life?*

Eventually, I came to understand that I had a divine appointment. So when I took a leap of faith in July 1986 to accept the position as VCS superintendent, I stepped into the greatest adventure of my life. Over the next thirty-plus years, God answered our prayers in the most remarkable ways and gave us a bigger and bolder vision than we could have imagined.

The Quest for Quality Education is a story of transformation, and an example of what can happen when Christians and people of good will introduce a culture of Light, Life, and Learning™ (described in the next chapter) into America's schools and beyond. That's the story I want to share in these pages: the story of what happens when parents, educators, and engaged community members vow to settle for nothing less than the best for the children in their schools.

CHAPTER 2

Raising Up a Standard:
Quest for Excellence
and a Moral Compass

THE QUEST FOR EXCELLENCE is never accidental. It comes only from diligence, perseverance, and a desire to perform at the highest level. This truth struck home for me at the start of the 1990–1991 school year. Over the summer I had read the book *In Search of Excellence: Lessons from America's Best-Run Companies*, by Thomas J. Peters and Robert H. Waterman Jr. The book prompted some serious contemplation about the nature of excellence, and deep down some very important dots connected for me.

For several years, I wrestled with the thought that many people, including many Christians, perceived Christian schools as substandard or second rate. Sadly, these folks were often right. But why did Christian schools, businesses, books, and movies all too frequently convey an image of mediocrity? Why would people of faith be willing to settle for less than the best when engaged in activities that should bring honor and glory to God?

It frustrated me how many dismissed Christian values as a joke. But the more I thought about it, I realized many believers tend to see themselves as underdogs in the social order. When secular culture sees biblical principles as old-fashioned or out-of-step, believers may decide that simply struggling along with poor finances and inferior quality is the price we have to pay for clinging to our values. As long as we're "doing our best" in difficult circumstances, it's easy to rationalize mediocre performance and claim it as our "spiritual sacrifice." But in matters of such magnitude, it's never okay to settle for less than excellence.

As that school year got underway, I began sharing my thoughts with everyone who would listen, from the VCS board members to our faculty, parents, community friends, and others. "God has provided all the resources we need to represent Him faithfully and reflect His glory," I said. "Why shouldn't Christians have the best schools, the finest art and literature, and the highest caliber people producing the best in every field?" History's greatest art, music, and literature came forth as the work of Christians. Believers laid the foundations of modern science in virtually every field. So what changed?

"God's resources are unlimited," I insisted. Before long, the redirection of focus began taking on a life of its own. I started calling the new emphasis the QUEST for Excellence. The definition of "excellence" became the key to the success of the venture. At Valley Christian Schools, we define the highest standard of excellence as the nature, character, and works of God. As we began implementing these ideas, we embarked on a journey toward God's excellence. While we understand that we can never fully attain true excellence this side of heaven, we believe the QUEST for Excellence leads naturally to the Quest for Quality Education.

As I saw it, the promise of quality education was Valley's best hope for improving our financial resources. VCS had faced daunting deficits for many years. Fundraising efforts reflected a crisis perspective: "Help us or we die!" That less-than-inspiring approach left some donors with the feeling of being manipulated for their dollars. Some people made donations with the attitude, "All right, I'll bail you out *again*, but would you please get your financial house in order and run the school with the same good business practices that all successful businesses follow?"

Contributions based on guilt and the threat of disaster brought no joy to the givers or us. But I knew if our donors became genuinely excited about a particular program or educational improvement, they would give joyfully from the heart. So I asked our administrators and department heads to think about the programs they would like to see offered in every department, and then pray God would give them "the desires of their hearts."

Based on the promise of Psalm 37:4, the idea was that God puts His desires into our hearts so He can achieve His purposes through us. I encouraged the department heads to stretch their faith, to imagine educational offerings so excellent and unique that people would say, "If you want that, you'll have to go to Valley Christian Schools."

We began challenging and preparing all of our students to discover and develop their God-given talents to emerge as excellent professionals with exceptional influence. The key to success lay in students committing to pursue excellence as a way of life with a determination to set high standards of achievement as future leaders in their communities. By shifting the focus of learning to the QUEST for Excellence, we believed new opportunities of influence in the community would naturally follow. We became convinced the school would attract more students with a cycle of systematic development, continuous improvement, and showcasing program opportunities with improved publications and public relations year after year.

The results were amazingly gratifying. Added revenue from increased enrollment enabled a cycle of new programs and continuous improvements. Better faculty salaries attracted better teachers, which in turn boosted educational quality as well as the demand for admissions. Along the way, we underwent a fundamental change of focus as we committed to becoming less school-centered and more customer-centered. I had long believed that parents are the primary educators of their children under God. This idea took on greater significance as we emphasized our conviction that the school exists to serve God by serving parents. And we serve our parents best by providing an excellent education for their children.

EXCELLENCE BRINGS INFLUENCE

Despite the substantial expense the QUEST for Excellence demanded, I've always had an unshakable belief that continuous improvement is non-negotiable for Valley Christian Schools. I came to believe the school's financial strength depended on the success of the QUEST for Excellence. As an added benefit, a focus on building extraordinary quality attracted more people of means who could afford to send their children to any school they chose. After enrolling their children, they often expressed higher expectations than our school programs could deliver. As a result, they often generously contributed toward continuous program development. They even began contributing to our Youth with Promise Fund that supports students whose parents could not otherwise afford to send their children to VCS.

None of this happened overnight, of course, and we had some huge barriers to overcome along the way. The unwavering support of the VCS board, including Dr. Rick Watson, who became board chair in 1991, was a critical factor in our continuous growth. Rick's passion for quality education impressed all of us from the moment he arrived, encouraging us to accomplish everything God intended.

The commitment to excellence in all aspects of our programs and curriculum didn't go unnoticed. The school became a topic of conversation in our community and beyond. Students from other schools began coming to us, asking to transfer to Valley. I received calls from business and community leaders curious about what was happening on the hill as we prepared to break ground on our new Skyway campus. With all the newfound attention, everyone saw how our "Excellence Brings Influence" motto was becoming a reality. People who might have ignored Valley Christian Schools at one time became friends and supporters.

As we responded to all these changes, I came to another realization: Professionals and institutions that insist on the highest standards have significant influence in shaping the conscience and character of their community and nation. Men and women we admire have an impact, one way or another, on our attitudes, beliefs, and behaviors. They influence the way we think and act, especially when it comes to our decisions regarding right and wrong. So our passion became expressed in a new question: "Shouldn't our students, as aspiring Christian professionals, be among the most influential people in our communities, helping to shape the moral conscience of our culture?"

Rather than engaging in the cultural dialogue and serving as "salt and light" (spoken of so eloquently by Jesus), too many misguided believers have chosen to escape from the world into their "holy huddles." But we had growing confidence that VCS ought to reject the mistaken idea that separation from the world is holiness unto God. Our school should not provide an escape from the world for our students but rather a powerful preparation to positively influence their communities and the world. We could see that excellence does indeed bring influence, and we were determined to train our students to engage the world through their personal quests for excellence.

In short, we decided to stop sheltering our students from the world. Instead, we wanted to prepare them to engage and transform culture with the shining light of "self-evident truths." We began challenging them to serve as excellent Christians, students, professionals, members of society, and ultimately men and women of influence. I became convinced that God is equipping a new generation of Christian youth with an understanding of His truth and a passion for positively impacting our world with their unique gifts and talents. And I was excited to think how Valley Christian Schools could be at the forefront of such transformation.

TO KNOW THE TRUTH

Our journey during the past several years in pursuit of quality education has been nothing short of amazing. We have connected with public schools, private schools in other parts of the country, and even with international schools. The primary means of reaching out to all these communities involves two dynamic programs, developed at Valley since 2006, called Junior University and the Lighthouse Initiative, abbreviated as the acronym JULI. These programs can extend the QUEST for Excellence and enable children to reach their full potential among all socioeconomic circumstances, schools, and educational organizations.

As we began crafting these programs, we were buoyed by the fact that the State of California Education Code, Section 233.5(a), requires instruction on patriotism and a moral code in the state's public schools. Character development is one of the most important learning objectives young people can achieve. Yet confusion about finding a common moral authority on which to teach right and wrong has often served to deter agreement about the teaching of a moral code. Thankfully, by working together with our local public school administrators and teachers, we've discovered that teaching children about the Declaration of Independence and the Common Virtues in the nation's founding document helps provide a moral authority and common foundation from which to address this mandate.

At Valley Christian Schools, we had strong evidence our programs were working for us, demonstrated daily in the lives of our students. The authority of our Christian faith serves us well as a moral compass and rudder for the character development of our students. As our local public school principals and I worked to help make the educational advantages of our students on the hill flow to the socio-economically disadvantaged students in the valley, we discussed how to set a comparable moral authority in place in our public schools. At first, it seemed like an impossible challenge since the endorsement of any religion within a public school is prohibited.

One thing we discovered as we began reaching out to the local schools: The truth is always the truth, whether it's expressed by Christians or by non-Christians, by Americans or by people from other countries. We have a remarkable cultural mix in our community, with many different ethnic groups, languages, religions, denominations, and perspectives about the meaning and purpose of life. And of course, some profess no religious faith at all. But the truth is still the truth no matter our varied and enriching cultures.

The Declaration of Independence states that we are all "created equal," that we are "endowed by [our] Creator with certain unalienable rights, that among these are life, liberty, and the pursuit of happiness." These truths pre-existed our nation's birth and were eloquently inscribed in our founding document and on the granite walls of our national monuments. I believe our Creator embedded these truths in the history of every nation. These are truths our children need to understand, and I can't imagine who would be more inspired to make such truths available to children than Christians and people of good will. Sharing these truths with the young people in our schools is the duty of every parent and educator.

Certainly, the Founders did not intend to imply equality of physical stature, wealth, knowledge, or years of good health. So what did they mean by saying we are all created equal? I contend that "created equal" means we are all equal with immense and incalculable value when viewed through the eyes of our Creator. This truth should shape how we view each other and ourselves.

These insights are a legacy of the Declaration of Independence for all people and for all time. While these ideas did not originate within our founding document, it affirms them as a birthright for all people. Understanding the value of our shared heritage can help to instill a culture of goodness, peace, and joy in our schools. While searching for a moral authority among our local public school leaders, we discovered the phrase "Common Virtues." That phrase and the timeless principles it represents became a strong foundation for character instruction. We can teach good character to all the children in all of our schools based upon the moral authority of Common Virtues.

Christian schools do not have an exclusive right to share these truths. Yes, we have greater freedom to speak with our students about issues of faith, but every teacher in every school has the freedom to teach the values, virtues, and beliefs stated in the Declaration of Independence. They are truths that generations of Americans have affirmed and defended. They are essential character-building tools.

BLIND SPOTS

Before we got very far in implementing the JULI programs in public schools, however, I had to deal with a couple of blind spots in my thinking. As we began thinking about how we could interact most effectively with our neighborhood schools, we wanted to be sure we wouldn't break any laws related to the issues of separation of church and state. Like a lot of Americans, I believed that the law of the land, ever since the controversial Supreme Court decisions of the 1960s, was that Bible reading and prayers are illegal in our public schools. The entire nation and I, it seemed, were convinced there was nothing we could do to reintroduce a Christian perspective as a positive influence in our schools. The courts had scrubbed prayers, student-led devotionals, and any mention of religion, we thought. As secular institutions, I reasoned, public schools were forced to deny moral instruction to avoid any form of religious bias. But I came to see how my beliefs were mistaken.

A related blind spot I discovered was my belief that, as Christian teachers and administrators, we could offer a Christian education only to the students who showed up at our doors. We could make a difference spiritually for students in our Christian schools, but the public schools were strictly off limits. Sadly, I think a lot of people have the same attitude about the children's programs in their churches. They say, "We can only take care of those who come to us, and we won't try to reach out to the rest of the young people in our community." But that's a mistake and a self-imposed limitation no Christian parent or educator should accept.

Our calling as educators should extend to all children in our community. As Christians or just as good citizens, we must help provide educational opportunities for every child, not just those who attend our Christian schools or churches. Moreover, the free exercise clause of the First Amendment ensures our right to "adopt" our neighborhood schools with programs such as Junior University and the Lighthouse Initiative.

As we began discussing the initial plan for JULI, officials from the nearby Franklin–McKinley School District asked their legal team to review our programs to ensure their compliance with all federal, state, and local laws. At the same time, we at Valley Christian Schools asked our legal counsel to offer an opinion.

Legal and judicial opinions turn on the establishment and free exercise clauses of the First Amendment to the U.S. Constitution, which read this way: "Congress shall make no law respecting an establishment of religion, or prohibiting the free exercise thereof." This means Congress has no authority to rule either for or against religion in any form.

What we discovered is that cooperative programs such as Junior University and the Lighthouse Initiative reside well within state and local guidelines and do not violate the establishment clause of the First Amendment to the Constitution. Rather, these programs enable Christians and people of good will to provide valuable resources when approved through the school leadership. You will read more later about the distinction between the speech and activities allowed during classroom sessions or other official school events and those permitted during student-led club gatherings and programs operating before or after school with parent permission. Knowing with confidence that these efforts have a secure constitutional footing based on the guarantees accorded by the First Amendment helped overcome the concerns about violating the time-proven principle of separation of church and state.

The simple fact is that all the children in our communities deserve to know the truths enshrined in our national charters. They need to hear how our rights come, not from government, but from our Creator, as the Declaration affirms. And they need to hear that they have equal value. Every boy and girl deserves an opportunity to learn about our great national heritage. And, during after-school programs with parent permission, Christians can legally share the stories and teachings of the Bible to allow every child to learn about Jesus and have a choice to follow Him.

TOWARD A BOLDER VISION

The QUEST for Excellence and the Quest for Quality Education are two sides of the same coin: a movement with the potential to transform the institutions shaping American culture in the 21st century and well beyond. Giving children opportunities to achieve educational excellence, mentoring them with applied learning, and training them in core values such as integrity, kindness, diligence, and mutual respect provide a solid foundation for those destined to take the reins of leadership.

The tent meetings of the 18th and 19th centuries in this country brought Christian faith to millions during the formation of the American character. The "Great Awakenings" of that era helped establish a sense of national conscience and a bond of good will that lasted for many years. I believe a renewed interest in faith and a commitment to the restoration of civil order in our cities and towns could have much the same impact today.

You don't have to look very far to see how this country is facing some monumental educational challenges. The cultural debate that began back in the 1960s remains as heated as ever. Yet amid all the controversy, the faithful legacy of our founding principles can have a positive influence to reshape our national education agenda. The Common Virtues, as expressed in the preamble to the Declaration of Independence, can help improve the culture of the nation's schools and the character of our youth for decades to come.

The Bible is full of examples of people God used to implement the Excellence Brings Influence strategy. Daniel and the three Hebrew youths whose stories appear in the book of Daniel were promoted to serve King Nebuchadnezzar because they had "intelligence in every branch of wisdom, endowed with understanding and discerning knowledge."[5] These young men became the most influential professionals in ancient Babylon because they refused to compromise their beliefs. They demanded excellence of themselves, and true excellence brings influence. As a result, they transformed their culture and brought respect for God to a pagan nation.

Daniel's influence was rooted in his excellent spirit, knowledge, and wisdom: "Then this Daniel was preferred above the presidents and princes because an excellent spirit was in him."[6] King Belshazzar said to Daniel, "I have heard of you, that the Spirit of God is in you, and that light and understanding and excellent wisdom are found in you."[7]

God's strategy was dramatically effective. He challenged, educated, transformed, and commissioned these young men to reflect His excellence to restore respect for the one true God in an otherwise godless nation. Other examples from Scripture show how God promoted people of excellent character to positions of influence to engage and transform their culture. These include Abraham, Moses, David, Nehemiah, the patriarch Joseph, Esther, and of course Mary and her husband, Joseph, who were chosen of God to impact the entire world and all of history. All of these people were chosen of God because they were people of excellence.

While the professions of these Bible characters varied widely, all were people through whom God worked greatly to achieve a powerful redemptive influence in the world. Each had a passion for reflecting the nature, character, and works of God. And people who pursue God's nature and character make themselves candidates to serve as conduits for the mighty works of God.

LIGHT, LIFE, AND LEARNING

I often use the phrase "Light, Life, and Learning" to describe the key components of every successful learning environment. Light comes from the "self-evident" truth that we are all "created equal" with unimaginable worth. The Light in this continuum illuminates the value of every person. Our schools must teach all students, as a foundation for a quality education, that they and every person are of equal and incredible value.

A single Bible reading on the topic reveals the origin of the idea of equality found in the Declaration of Independence. The passage appears in the first chapter of the Bible, declaring, "So God created human beings in his own image. In the image of God he created them; male and female he created them."[8] This truth is foundational and critically important for restoring academic excellence in America's schools, especially where children feel unimportant and unvalued.

The cruel "survival of the fittest" mentality is at best depersonalizing and at worst deadly. In the absence of Light, the truth does not appear, and darkness prevails. In the absence of Light, our precious children often feel unworthy and disrespected when compared to others. The resulting struggle for significance inevitably leads to terrible consequences, including playground fights, cyber-bullying, gangs, depression, a sense of hopelessness, suicides and—as we have witnessed all too often—even once unimaginable events such as school shootings. Academic achievement, of course, becomes severely impaired in such a morbid and depersonalized school culture.

Life proceeds from Light and involves the realization that every man, woman, and child has a purpose and a destiny. The Declaration of Independence affirms every person's equal value and God-given right to pursue life, liberty, and happiness.

The sequence of Light, Life, and Learning is important, because light precedes life, and life precedes learning. Maybe it would help to think of growing plants. First, sun**light** warms and energizes the earth, allowing seeds below the soil to germinate and sprout to **life**. As the plants emerge from the soil, they begin to grow and thrive, and with life-giving rain, the plants produce a good harvest, an appropriate metaphor for fruitful **learning**.

We've found that the principles of the Light, Life, and Learning continuum help to create an emotional readiness in students to learn. Too often educators fail to achieve academic success because the Light and Life have not sufficiently prepared their students for Learning. When the sequence successfully takes place, the pace of learning accelerates exponentially as these ideas take root in the minds and hearts of our students. The Light, Life, and Learning paradigm has helped to transform the public school culture in our local neighborhood. The public elementary school principals where we began the JULI program adopted the phrase "goodness, peace, and joy" to describe the emerging school culture at their schools.

The initial efforts at Hellyer Elementary School to reverse declining achievement scores graphically confirmed the critical importance of the Life, Light, and Learning paradigm. In the hope of improving learning, the faculty and school leaders agreed to remove all aspects of the curriculum except the minimum State requirements and to focus only on language and math. The results were completely unexpected. The achievement scores dropped, and learning was depressed even more. Why? Because children need Light, Life, and Learning, and in that order. Shortcuts to learning are always doomed to disappointment, as occurred at Hellyer Elementary School. Thankfully, the school leadership took a complete turn toward the Light, Life, and Learning paradigm. After implementing the JULI program, Hellyer Elementary School progressed from being a school on state academic probation to becoming an exemplary school of distinction.

NEUTRALITY IS NOT HOSTILITY

After an in-depth study of American democracy during the 1830s, the French writer and historian Alexis de Tocqueville concluded, "Liberty cannot be established without morality, nor morality without faith."[9] In our time, when asked if government schools should be relied upon to teach their children Christian faith, almost all Christians agree with the high court's rulings against government-taught religion in public schools. So the question arises, "How can moral values and character development be taught in the public schools when the courts have barred the government schools from teaching students about the Bible, prayer, and even the Ten Commandments?"

Take a look at the Supreme Court's ruling in *Abington Township School District v. Schempp* (1963), in which Justice Tom C. Clark concluded the majority opinion by writing:

> The place of religion in our society is an exalted one, achieved through a long tradition of reliance on the home, the church and the inviolable citadel of the individual heart and mind. We have come to recognize through bitter experience that it is not within the power of government to invade that citadel, whether its purpose or effect be to aid or oppose, to advance or retard. In the relationship between man and religion, the State is firmly committed to a position of neutrality.[10]

In light of this and similar rulings, we have to wonder if we haven't misunderstood and overreacted to the Court's position. Neutrality about religious instruction does not imply overt hostility. Our problem began when Christians threw up our hands in despair, thinking the Supreme Court gave a final word to close the door to all Christian influence in our schools. For too long, Christians have suffered under the delusion that the Court's rulings mean there is nothing we can do to reach the children in our public schools with the love of Jesus. The Lighthouse model proves differently, as you will see. Our failure as believers to let the light of Jesus shine through us has resulted in an abandonment of almost all Christian influence on children in our schools.

Christian influence enjoyed a continuous presence in America's schools for about 350 years—ever since the founding of Plymouth Colony in 1620. Since 1962 and 1963, when the Supreme Court issued two opinions regarding government-directed prayer and Bible reading in public schools, the nation has undergone dramatic changes leading to an explosion of unintended consequences. A precipitous rise in vandalism, truancy, drug use, teen pregnancy, bullying, gun violence, murder, and suicide are among the heartbreaking results.[11]

This breakdown of moral values certainly can't be blamed entirely or even primarily on court decisions to prohibit government schools from leading students in prayer and Bible readings. I believe our failure as people of faith to support our schools has contributed to a decreasing Christian influence in education. The sad outcomes include a dramatic decline in academic achievement among many of our youth. There are too many statistics confirming the poor performance in a majority of our public schools to pretend we don't have a problem.

FOUNDING FAITH

The American public school system originated in one-room schoolhouses and churches all across the country, where, with rare exceptions, educators integrated Christian faith throughout the curriculum. Textbooks like the *McGuffey Readers* emphasized biblical terms and principles, in part because the Bible was such a prominent feature in virtually every American home. Its principles offered a moral compass and rudder for those who applied the "love your neighbor as yourself" equity and truth messages of the Bible to social injustices, including slavery and institutional racism, that partly remain in this 21st century.

Regarding the character of American schooling at that time, Tocqueville concluded, "Almost all education is entrusted to the clergy."[12] And he added, "Christianity, which has declared that all men are equal in the sight of God, will not refuse to acknowledge that all citizens are equal in the eye of the law."[13] Tocqueville indeed expressed the high moral view evident in the Declaration of Independence, which helped shape the founding of our nation.

Reflecting on these thoughts, I decided one Saturday to put aside my usual weekend activities to read the Declaration of Independence without interruption. The soaring prose of the document, signed on July 4, 1776, is as inspirational today as more than 240 years ago. As I considered the power of these founding words, it occurred, it occurred to me that I had never really appreciated the substance of this magnificent document. And nowhere were the author's words more potent than in the concluding paragraph, which proclaimed:

> We, therefore, the Representatives of the United States of America, in General Congress, Assembled, appealing to the Supreme Judge of the world for the rectitude of our intentions, do, in the Name, and by Authority of the good People of these Colonies, solemnly publish and declare, That these united Colonies are, and of Right ought to be Free and Independent States; that they are Absolved from all Allegiance to the British Crown, and that all political connection between them and the State of Great Britain, is and ought to be totally dissolved; and that as Free and Independent States, they have full Power to levy War, conclude Peace, contract Alliances, establish Commerce, and to

do all other Acts and Things which Independent States may of right do. And for the support of this Declaration, with a firm reliance on the protection of divine Providence, we mutually pledge to each other our Lives, our Fortunes and our sacred Honor.

After reading their Declaration, I pondered how the first citizens of the United States of America dared to risk their lives and fortunes as they confronted the mightiest army on Earth. The thought came to me: *If they appealed "to the Supreme Judge of the world for the rectitude of [their] intentions . . . with a firm reliance on the protection of divine Providence," we ought to be willing to do no less on behalf of the children in our schools.*

The word "rectitude" in that powerful phrase means uprightness, righteousness, and correctness in judgment, indeed, an appropriate basis of morality in our schools. This legacy is part of the treasure to which all Americans are entitled. The buried treasure of moral authority, enabling students to discern right from wrong, can be rediscovered and reinstated in all of our schools by teaching and honoring the Declaration of Independence.

A CHANGE OF PERSPECTIVE

For perspective, it is helpful to consider the disruptions that took place as a result of the high court's rulings in the early 1960s. Americans have seldom faced a more hotly debated topic than the injunctions against Bible reading and prayer during school hours. In *Engel v. Vitale* (1962), the Supreme Court ruled that New York schools could no longer require students to recite a prayer composed by the local school board. The following year, in *Abington Township School District v. Schempp* (1963), the Court ruled that school-sponsored Bible reading and recitation of the Lord's Prayer were unconstitutional.

Suddenly, Bible reading and prayer were forbidden in public schools, giving many the perception that these activities were dubious and unacceptable. Based on what many considered a biased and inaccurate reading of the First Amendment to the U.S. Constitution, the ban left many Christian parents with a sense of isolation because of the incompatibility of their values with the secular bias of the Court. These parents saw their only options as turning to private education or homeschooling their children. Since that time, millions of families have abandoned the public schools. Many, with a sense of righteous anger, feel the schools and the government deserve terrible public education because they "expelled God from public schools."

The most recent U.S. Department of Education information indicates that parents now homeschool about two million students or about 3.4 percent of all K–12 students, an increase from slightly over one million or 2.2 percent in 2003. Ninety-one percent of homeschooling parents cited their concern about the environment in the schools as the main or one of the main reasons for their decision to homeschool, and seventy-seven percent said they preferred to provide moral instruction for their children at home.[14]

Other families sacrifice to pay tuition at private religious or non-sectarian schools to provide an education consistent with their faith and academic standards. Predictably, government school compliance with the Supreme Court's mandates, combined with the exodus of families concerned about low academic standards, has had a detrimental impact on the public schools in most cities and towns. Without any framework to establish a moral compass and rudder, and with no commonly accepted standards for teaching lessons about virtue and good character, many public schools find themselves hard-pressed to deal with serious behavioral problems.

Like many Americans, I thought the public schools were doomed to low quality because the Supreme Court stripped away the moral authority for the light and life that prepare students for learning. But I began to wonder if we might find a way to reintroduce the Light, Life, and Learning continuum back into our public school instruction. *Indeed,* I thought, *there must be a way for the schools to tap into the legacy of our nation's Founders.*

CHAPTER 3

AN EXPANDING VISION:
BRINGING RESOURCES AND HOPE

THE STORY OF THE JUNIOR UNIVERSITY program
at Valley Christian Schools began with a visit to my office in the fall
of 2006 by Sheilah Lane, then principal of Hellyer Elementary School,
along with Liz Nandakumar, then a resource specialist at Hellyer and
a Valley parent. Our school sits on a hilltop with a commanding view
of Silicon Valley, and Hellyer Elementary is located right below us.
Principal Lane described some of the challenges she and her staff
faced. Despite their best efforts, she said, the teachers at Hellyer were
struggling amidst a lack of resources, with little expectation things
would ever improve.

While working at Hellyer, Liz would often look up the hill toward
the VCS campus and wonder if our school could join her elementary
school in a mentoring partnership to improve learning opportunities for Hellyer's students. She posed the question to Claude Fletcher,
serving as Valley's chancellor at the time, and their brief discussion
led to the meeting in my office a week or so later.

Listening to Principal Lane describe the problems at Hellyer, I
felt a strong desire to do something to help. We learned that a high

percentage of the kids there were failing academically. Many were English language learners whose parents spoke only another language at home. Teaching children to read a language they could barely speak seemed like an impossible task. Furthermore, we learned that seventy-two percent of the 460 families with children at Hellyer had severe economic challenges.

Because of the students' low performance on the mandatory annual standardized achievement exams, the state had placed Hellyer on academic probation. The Academic Performance Index (API), used by public schools at that time to measure school-wide performance, labeled scores below 800 as unacceptable. Hellyer's average API score was 756 and falling.

When Principal Lane shared her concerns, she asked a most unexpected question: Would it be possible for student volunteers from our high school to go down the hill to tutor, mentor, and inspire the students at Hellyer during the school day? "The younger children will listen to your kids," she said, "and it could be a life-changing opportunity for them." Her request surprised us. Even though we sympathized with Hellyer's situation, I couldn't help but think of all the risks and limitations involved.

I felt we ought to do something, but releasing our students away from their studies during the school day didn't seem possible, I reasoned. Even providing transportation back and forth between the schools would pose a problem. Besides, VCS is a Christian school, and everybody knew about the "wall of separation" between Christian and public schools—or so we thought. I mentioned some of the hurdles we would have to overcome, but Sheilah Lane remained unwavering. Before the conversation ended, I promised to think further about her request, and I agreed to allow her to try recruiting Valley students to serve as tutoring mentors of her students, even though I had no idea what such a program might entail.

Principal Lane was persuasive. She recruited a handful of students for a limited tutoring program during the 2006–2007 school year. But our class schedules at Valley prohibited effective time on task with Hellyer students during the school day, and Hellyer's average API score continued to decline, falling to 736. When Mrs. Lane came back to speak to us about her predicament, I challenged our high school principal, Dr. Joel Torode, and his leadership team to find some way to coordinate the high school schedule to allow our students to volunteer at Hellyer during the school day. It took a bit of creative thinking and a reorganization of class schedules, but they managed to do it for the good of all the involved students at both schools.

During the 2007–2008 school year, thirty VCHS students began making the trip down to Hellyer Elementary for about three hours per week to mentor the younger children. Having secured 3,060 hours of student volunteer time, Principal Lane thought the new program ought to have a name, and she's the one who dubbed it Junior University. She believed our college-bound juniors and seniors would help improve student learning at Hellyer and, in the process, inspire her students to set their own goals to attend college.

It was a brilliant plan. Junior University offered enormous benefits for everyone concerned, Hellyer students and ours. Valley Christian's buses eventually made hundreds of student trips per week,[15] ferrying our "Junior University professors" to tutor the children at Hellyer Elementary.

EXTENDING OUR HORIZONS

Now the program was in place with everyone on board. Even though remedial educational programs have a history of disappointment, I still hoped ours would succeed. Nevertheless, the 2008 API scores stunned everyone. Hellyer's average API score for 2008 had advanced fifty-seven points, from a base of 736 the previous year to a new high of 793.

The internet home page of the Franklin–McKinley School District, of which Hellyer is a part, reported the results with well-deserved pride, giving praise and thanks to the Valley high school students who had donated their time and talents.

After dropping back a few points in 2009, Hellyer achieved a 2010 API score of 808 while meeting growth targets in all subgroups, including Asian, Hispanic or Latino, socioeconomically disadvantaged, and English learners. Everyone celebrated, and Hellyer Elementary got released from the state's academic probation. Shortly after hearing these results, District Superintendent Dr. John Porter invited Cindy Nardi, VCHS's Junior University director, and me to attend a Franklin–McKinley School District board meeting where members expressed their appreciation for our students' good work.

In the fall of 2011, VCHS began its fifth year offering the full Junior University program. Along the way, we developed a great relationship with Jerry Merza, who had succeeded Sheilah Lane as principal of Hellyer Elementary School after her retirement in 2009.

By 2013, with an API score of 828, Hellyer became one of the highest performing elementary schools in Santa Clara County among those with a student population at or above the region's average of twenty-three percent "Spanish-speaking English language learners." Even including charter schools, Hellyer ranked fifth in all of Santa Clara and San Mateo Counties. The API data clearly showed a significant increase in test scores for the mentored group of students as measured on a year-to-year basis.

As you can imagine, our team rejoiced at the success of Junior University. Dr. Stephen McMinn, then the chief operating officer at VCS, produced a separate statistical analysis demonstrating the differences in achievement between the Hellyer students who were mentored by VCHS students and those not mentored. He used the study as the basis of his doctoral dissertation. Both groups were randomly selected, and the results of the study were astounding. After analysis of all the data, the contrast between the two groups impressed everyone. The likelihood that the improvement shown by students in the mentored groups had occurred by random chance was less than one in ten-thousand.

Perhaps most amazing of these results was that the Junior University program reached the majority of children who had never shown any potential for academic success. Students were invited to take part in the program, and when they discovered they could succeed and become recognized for their efforts, they were thrilled. The opportunity transformed their lives in profound ways. Formerly low-achieving students began performing at much higher levels in all their subjects.

These kids had real potential, but they had been using their talents in the wrong ways. As in many of the public schools in Silicon Valley, the Hellyer students faced plenty of less than desirable options. Even in elementary school, some children were involved with gangs, drugs, and other dangers. They could see where their lives would end up if they didn't change directions. But thanks to the volunteer mentors of Junior University, they met the kind of people they wanted to become.

A CONVERSATION WITH GOD

After some years of offering the Junior University program, a huge disparity came to my attention. The contrast between the exceptional co-curricular resources available to Valley Christian students and the limited resources at Hellyer became acutely obvious. Students at Hellyer didn't have a single music teacher, but Valley Christian had an outstanding Conservatory of the Arts. They didn't have an art teacher, a dance teacher, or a robotics program at any level. Hellyer didn't have any of the programs and opportunities that were making such a difference for our students. State budget constraints and other hurdles still seriously hampered the school. The teachers were stretched thin and had very little time for working with the children who needed the most help. Even less time existed to help those who could easily become high achievers with more assistance.

One cold morning in January 2012, the plight of Hellyer Elementary School weighed heavily on my mind as I drove to work, so I complained to God. "It's not fair!" I said aloud. "The Hellyer students deserve the same opportunities as Valley Christian students." Like many believers, I had for the most part written off the public schools as hopeless. Junior University, with hands-on mentoring of Hellyer students by hundreds of our high school students, had helped the public school children improve their core curricular academic skills over the past four years, but there had to be more.

The seeming finality of the judicial decisions forbidding prayer and Bible reading in the public schools troubled me, so I reasoned with God: "The Court's rulings are insurmountable barriers to restoring Christian values in the public schools. The judicial system has walled off the most important opportunities for character development for these children. I have no idea how to teach children the importance of good character and moral restraint without teaching them about the Bible and how to pray. And that's forbidden by the Supreme Court."

I continued, "Lord, it's great the Christian schools have the privilege of teaching children about You, but the children at Hellyer Elementary School are just as precious to You as the children at our school. Sadly, the doors of the public schools are shut and padlocked to the Christian virtues that gave birth to our nation."

No sooner had I lodged my complaint than I sensed an immediate reply from the Lord: *So you think the highest law in the land is the United States Supreme Court?* The unexpected response stunned me, so I backpedaled as fast as I could. "Oh, no! I'm sorry, Lord. Please forgive my lack of faith. I know You are the Supreme Judge of the Supreme

Court of the heavens and the earth." Several seconds passed, and then I felt the Lord speaking to me again: *If you believe the Supreme Court of the heavens and the earth is truly the highest court in the land, then why don't you put the rulings of the Supreme Court of the United States on appeal to Me? I will take the case.*

My conversation with the Creator and Supreme Judge of the universe rattled me. But even without knowing how to respond to His offer, I was excited to think God was aware of our concerns and even more interested in reaching public school children than I was. So the next Tuesday evening, I shared the events of that morning with our VCS prayer intercessors at our weekly prayer meeting in my office.

Each member of the prayer team listened intently. Then we made an earnest appeal to the Supreme Court Judge of the heavens and the earth to "judge righteously, and defend the rights of the afflicted and needy"[16] by reversing or at least minimizing the effects resulting from the rulings of the Supreme Court of the United States regarding religious liberty in the nation's schools.

From that moment on, a metamorphosis began taking place in my understanding of the law. God overturned many of my misconceptions about the rulings of the U.S. Supreme Court. The actions of the Court had in no way stopped God's ability to do His work for students at Hellyer Elementary or any other public school. As our understanding grew, our prayers matured. We prayed God would help Christians realize the legal right of public school children to learn from the Bible and pray so that they could thrive with Light, Life, and Learning in a school culture of goodness, peace, and joy. We wondered how God would do such a marvelous thing, but we became convinced He would.

PRAYERS FOR THE PUBLIC SCHOOLS

After my surprise conversation with the Lord, the prayer intercessors and I began praying about how God might use VCS as a model to help students everywhere to embrace the Common Virtues Initiative. Dr. Ed Silvoso, the founder of Harvest Evangelism, Transform Our World, and the International Transformation Network, serves as our school's board chaplain. In early 2012, Ed asked if I would like to give the keynote address at the Global Transform Our World conference in Hawaii the following October. I hadn't anticipated the invitation, but I was honored and said I would give Ed's request some serious thought. I would need some time to think about what I had to share.

Dr. Silvoso had asked to produce a documentary about Valley Christian Schools, and I agreed. Filming began on Monday, January 23, and progressed well. But during the video shoot at Hellyer Elementary featuring Junior University, I heard the grim news that Principal Merza's wife, Lyn, had been diagnosed with ovarian cancer. The malignancy had advanced to Stage IIIC. The survival rate of five years or longer for ovarian cancer patients at that stage was frighteningly low—a reported thirty-five percent. My heart went out to Jerry, Lyn, and their children. The thought of three-year-old Brayden and his fourth-grade sister, Cameron, losing their mother was devastating.

When the VCS intercessors and I prayed for Lyn, I had a strong sense of God's leading to invite Jerry to lunch and ask if our students could pray for his wife. Honestly, I felt awkward asking him that question since I didn't know how he might respond. Nevertheless, Jerry and I scheduled our lunch meeting, and we had a pleasant meal as I waited for the right time to ask. Jerry's answer put me at ease.

"I appreciate the offer, Cliff. But let me ask Lyn if she would like to meet with your students for prayer." Several weeks passed without an answer from Jerry, and I began to wonder whether it would ever happen. I finally concluded, *We'll have to wait. It's in God's hands.*

As it turned out, my offer of prayer set in motion a wonderful sequence of events. Along with Cindy Nardi, director of Junior University, our intercessors and I had been praying for an opportunity to provide an after-school Kids Club at Hellyer Elementary, with parental consent, where the public school children could hear Bible stories, sing Christian songs, and learn how to pray and follow Jesus.

When the Junior University program began during the 2006–2007 school year, Hellyer Elementary did not allow an after-school Kids Club, out of concerns rooted in the establishment clause of the First Amendment. Even though we were disappointed, we prayed for the opportunity for a Kids Club, because "with God all things are possible."[17]

PRAYER IN THE CLASSROOM

After several years of denied requests for a Kids Club at Hellyer, Cindy Nardi and I discussed whether Valley Christian High School should continue to invest our student capital in the Junior University program. We decided we should do all we could to help Hellyer students on whatever terms the administration offered. So our request became, "Just tell us how we can help you, and we'll do our best to serve."

With that attitude of service, our relationship, trust, and friendship with the Hellyer administration and staff continued to grow. We weren't certain whether we would ever have a Kids Club at Hellyer, but we knew we were having a positive impact on the wonderful children at Hellyer. And as our high school students served them, all of us fell more and more in love with them.

Along the way, we made a wonderful discovery: Our courts have ruled that with parent permission, community volunteers may teach all children to pray and study the Bible during volunteer- or student-led programs before or after school. And, schoolchildren can legally read the Bible, pray, and share their faith during high school approved Christian club meetings. I was amazed to discover that the courts and Congress have ruled more than twice as often for protecting the religious freedoms of students, Bible study groups, and

Christian organizations in our schools than they have ruled to limit public schools from establishing religion-based programs. We have summarized six points:

1. Public schools may not conduct government sanctioned Bible readings and prayer.

2. Students have First Amendment religious rights that schools cannot deny at the schoolhouse gate.

3. Schools may not discriminate against any students who wish to conduct meetings for religious, political, or other speech.

4. School districts may not prohibit Bible study groups from meeting on school premises if other groups meet on school premises.

5. School districts may not exclude an adult-inspired club based on religious content. The First Amendment requires neutrality toward, not hostility against, a religious perspective.

6. If a district allows other community-based organizations to distribute similar information, then it cannot refuse distribution of literature advertising an off-campus summer program because it is taught from a Christian perspective.

The following chart lists the court and congressional rulings for the above six points:

COURT CASE OR LEGISLATION	ISSUE	FIRST AMENDMENT CLAUSE
Engel v. Vitale, Supreme Court, 1962	Government-directed prayer in public schools violates the establishment clause of the First Amendment	**Establishment Clause** Congress shall make no law respecting an establishment of religion,
Abington Township School District v. Schempp, Supreme Court, 1963	Sanctioned and organized Bible reading in public schools in the United States is unconstitutional	**Establishment Clause** Congress shall make no law respecting an establishment of religion,
Tinker v. Des Moines Independent Community School District, Supreme Court, 1969	Students have First Amendment rights that cannot be denied at the "schoolhouse gate"	**Free Exercise Clause** or prohibiting the free exercise thereof
Congress – Equal Access Act, 1984	Schools may not discriminate against any students who wish to conduct meetings ... for religious, political ... or other ... speech	**Free Exercise Clause** or prohibiting the free exercise thereof
Westside School District v. Mergens, Supreme Court, 1990	School districts may not prohibit Bible study groups from meeting on school premises if other groups meet on school premises	**Free Exercise Clause** or prohibiting the free exercise thereof
Good News Club v. Milford Central School District, Supreme Court, 2001	A district may not exclude an adult-initiated club on the basis of religious content. The First Amendment requires neutrality toward, not hostility against, a religious perspective	**Free Exercise Clause** or prohibiting the free exercise thereof
Hills v. Scottsdale Unified School District, 9th Circuit Court of Appeals, 329 F.3d. 1044, 2003	If a district allows other organizations to distribute similar information, then it cannot refuse distribution of literature advertising an off-campus summer program because it is taught from a Christian perspective	**Free Exercise Clause** or prohibiting the free exercise thereof

A broad understanding of these decisions offers good news for Christians who wish to teach Bible stories and pray with children before or after school with parent permission. And certainly, voluntary student attendance at a student-led Christian club during school is well within the framework of the law. The free exercise clause of the First Amendment guarantees these rights.

Although Hellyer Elementary, during our first five years of Junior University, had not allowed our students to lead an after-school Kids Club Bible program, we continued to wait and pray that God might open the door, even as we pressed on with our full support of our mentoring partnership.

Meanwhile, I became concerned about whether I had overstepped my bounds by asking Jerry Merza if our students could pray for his wife. It had been weeks since we'd spoken, so it was a pleasant surprise when Jerry called and told me Lyn had decided she did want to meet with our students to pray for her healing. I wanted to be sensitive to his situation, so I proposed, "If you're uneasy about the Supreme Court rulings forbidding prayer in public schools, our students would be glad to meet with Lyn on our campus if you think that best." But Jerry replied, "No, I want them to pray at my school." That was a surprise, but I quickly concurred. "Great, that will be fine." I immediately reflected on the words I had sensed during my conversation with God: *If you believe the Supreme Court of the heavens and the earth is truly the highest court in the land, then why don't you put the rulings of the Supreme Court of the United States on appeal to Me? I will take the case.* Then I remembered the words of the man who came to Jesus wanting Him to heal his son: "Lord, I believe; help my unbelief!"[18]

Thursday, April 19, 2012, between 2 and 3 p.m. was the time Jerry requested for us to meet and pray for Lyn. When I arrived at Hellyer, I learned that Mr. Merza reluctantly had had to reschedule his calendar to deal with urgent and unexpected principal duties. *Oh, no. What a shame,* I thought: *Jerry can't join us for prayer.* A few moments later, Lyn came into the office wearing a red scarf over her head, which I presumed meant she had lost hair as a result of her recent chemo treatments. I could see her apprehension, but she was smiling and friendly, although disappointed Jerry could not join us.

As we filed into the classroom, I think we all felt a warm sense of compassion for Lyn. A total of thirty-six people filled the room, including twenty-nine VCHS students, three VCS adult staff, Lyn's three-year-old son, Brayden, and her friend, Mylene. With Jesus in the midst of the group, those present were thirty-seven persons.[19]

Our high school students took turns praying for Lyn as she sat in a chair next to her son, who was sitting on Mylene's lap. The students prayed fervently for nearly an hour, and then it was a privilege for me to pray for Lyn as well. In closing, we implored God that our prayer in the Hellyer Elementary School classroom would open doors for a growing movement of prayer in public schools across the nation and to other parts of the world. And we all agreed with a hearty Amen.

After the prayers, little Brayden held his mother's hand as we walked back to the office. What a huge difference we believed our prayers would make for Lyn and her young family as God answered our petitions. I prayed earnestly that mother and son would be able to walk together, hand in hand, forever.

LONG-TERM DIVIDENDS

Back in the principal's office, I found Jerry wrapping up his duties. I decided it was time to pose the question I was considering: "Jerry, I've been invited to give the education keynote at the Global Transform Our World conference in Hawaii this October. Would you be willing to come and help as a co-speaker? So many wonderful improvements are happening at Hellyer. Your school is becoming a model to help other schools improve. I hope you'll be able to come, and it would be great if your family could come as well."

I paused for a moment as Jerry looked at me, wide-eyed. Then I added, "Let's all go to Hawaii. . . . We will take care of the expenses." He was surprised, but he answered quickly. "I'd be happy to help with the keynote, but Lyn and I will need to discuss whether or not to take the whole family." Not long after that conversation, Jerry called to tell me that Lyn and their whole family were making plans to attend the conference. We all hoped Lyn would be cancer free by then.

By this time, everyone saw Junior University as a great success. Hellyer students were meeting or exceeding the overall API-score achievement goals. Now we wanted to begin restoring the enrichment programs long ago removed by severe budget cuts. With hundreds of Valley Christian High School mentors eager to serve, Jerry Merza and the VCS Outreach Director, Cindy Nardi, plotted a course in late April and May 2012 to launch a sports, art, and music club (called the SAM Club) in the fall for the upcoming school year. Moreover, God answered our prayers, and we were soon granted permission to begin the Bible-based Kids Club at Hellyer that fall.

The VCHS volunteers enthusiastically disembarked from their buses at the Hellyer campus multiple times each week. We provided bus transportation for our student mentors without one dollar of expense to Hellyer Elementary or the Franklin–McKinley School District. Junior University continued as a completely non-religious academic mentoring program during the school day, while the SAM Club, Kids Club, and other Lighthouse electives served students after school. With parental permission, each Lighthouse mentoring opportunity was free to incorporate Bible stories, songs, or prayer. These kinds of programs have been tested repeatedly in the courts, and they are not only legal but encouraged in schools all across America.

Since my "It's not fair!" prayer on that cold January morning not so many months earlier, the Supreme Court Judge of the heavens and the earth had ruled in our favor, opening doors faster than I would ever have imagined. Although five years had passed from the time we began serving at Hellyer until the opportunity arose to launch the Bible club and the Lighthouse Initiative, it was well worth the wait. *What if we had quit serving after just a few years of service because we weren't able to start a Kids Club?* I pondered.

The next summer in 2013, we initiated "Splish! Splash! Learn to Swim," a summer swim program offered at the pool on our Skyway campus for first-, second-, and third-grade youngsters whose parents can't afford lessons. We learned there's an eighty percent reduction in the risk of drowning in a person's lifetime if they get swimming lessons, so we wanted to ensure every child in our local public schools could learn to swim and be safe around water. When we discussed the idea with the local public school principals, we got a favorable response. Under the umbrella of the Lighthouse Initiative, "Splish! Splash!" includes Bible lessons and prayer with parental permission.

Our program would work in a home pool or any place where children have safe access to a body of water. Christians and other people of good will in any community can make sure their neighborhood children learn how to swim. That's such a valuable contribution to the community. And with parent permission, they can share the good news of the gospel at the same time.

The benefits of this dynamic combination we call JULI (Junior University and the Lighthouse Initiative) were phenomenal. As a result of their success, five more public schools with students enrolled in kindergarten through twelfth grade began participating in JULI.

You will hear more about the development of Junior University and the Lighthouse Initiative from Jerry Merza's perspective in Chapter Five. But there's another program that has expanded in incredible ways to benefit and motivate thousands of children far beyond our own Silicon Valley neighborhood. The Quest for Space initiative is another amazing story.

THE QUEST FOR SPACE

During an AMSE Advisory Board brainstorming session, Dan Saldana shared his idea for an applied math, science, and engineering student project. I'll never forget his first sentence: "I'll help the students put a satellite in space." With that, he looked around the room to gauge interest in his idea. Everyone in the room seemed to push "pause," and I thought, *This is a high school, Dan, not NASA!* But eventually I managed to say, "Are you serious? How could VCS afford to put a satellite in space?"

At that point, Dan began describing his aerospace background. "During my career working with NASA at Lockheed, I headed eighty-nine satellite projects. Most of them were secret projects for the Defense Department. When I retired, I wanted to give back, so I offered to teach science and math in our public schools, but I discovered I needed a teaching credential. While I was looking around for the fastest way to get a teaching credential, I got a call from Bob Twiggs, a professor at Stanford University. He asked if I would like to work with him at Stanford to help students develop satellites."

Dan told us Bob Twiggs had co-invented the CubeSat, a miniaturized satellite for space research with a volume of exactly one liter (ten centimeters cubed). The CubeSat typically uses commercial off-the-shelf components for its electronics and weighs just under three pounds. Dan agreed to work with Professor Twiggs on the project to help Stanford students develop and fly payload modules of similar design called CubeLabs aboard the International Space Station (ISS). He was pleased with the arrangement, especially since Stanford didn't think he needed a teaching credential.

Bob Twiggs is now a Stanford professor emeritus and concurrently serves as a professor of astronautical engineering at Morehead State University and the University of Idaho. In 2010, *SpaceNews* named Professor Twiggs as one of the year's ten most influential space scientists, along with Elon Musk, CEO of SpaceX and Tesla Motors, and others. With that level of support for Dan and his accomplishments at NASA, we knew Dan was on to something.

"As I've been sitting here thinking about what I could offer AMSE students," Dan added, "I realized there's no reason why we can't put together a team of really bright and motivated students at Valley Christian to put a satellite into space."

It's a rare occasion, but I was speechless. After gathering my thoughts, I said, "If Stanford doesn't think you need a teaching credential, Dan, I think you will be well qualified to teach at Valley Christian High School."

But as soon as I said it, I had to ask the money question: "How much will it cost to launch a satellite?"

"Getting aboard a scheduled launch is the key," he replied. "At Stanford, we brought the cost down to $100,000, and I think we can lower that even more."

Hearing that, I had an astounding thought: *VCS is headed for space!*

FIRST HIGH SCHOOL CUBELABS IN SPACE

When Dan Saldana promised to recruit Professor Bob Twiggs to help launch Valley Christian High School's AMSE program, I was both amazed and apprehensive. But less than three months after Dan made the offer, Professor Twiggs and Dan Saldana came to my office with options for how VCHS could become the first high school in the world to put student-designed and student-developed CubeLab science experiments on the International Space Station.

Within twenty hours, Jeffery Manber, managing director of NanoRacks, presented a contract for launching the world's first high school CubeLab science experiment on the ISS. After a fast legal review, I signed it. NanoRacks would provide the interface with NASA and the ride to the ISS. Our students would design, fabricate, and build the CubeLab from scratch, and that was key.

Our students chose a plant growth experiment, researching which plants would work best in the microgravity environment. They installed an internal camera and many sensors to document stages of growth during the experiment. Astronauts on the ISS would "plug in" the CubeLab's USB outputs to their laptops to download the data to students at VCHS. And that was how our program began.

The AMSE Institute kicked off the 2010 school year with a bang, or, more accurately, a blastoff. VCS students met their biggest challenge with their successful design, fabrication, building, testing, and launch of the nation's first high school–designed CubeLab science experiment. The project launched into space in late January 2011 on the HTV-2 Japanese cargo spacecraft, boarded the International Space Station, and hitched a ride back to Earth in mid-March aboard the Russian Soyuz vehicle, riding on an astronaut's lap.

The next page in this story might be the most exciting. One of our distinguished AMSE Advisory Board members accompanied me as we made a trip to Coalinga, California, to ask Principal Tara Davis if Faith Christian Academy (FCA), with only about two dozen high school students, would consider the challenge of putting an experiment on the ISS.

Mrs. Davis didn't hesitate, confirming how God does big things in small places. This little school partnered with VCS to do something unprecedented and normally unthinkable. Twenty-four Faith Christian Academy high school students put a Level III (the most challenging) science experiment on a rocket to the International

Space Station, and their amazing accomplishment proved even small schools can achieve big dreams. They later received a letter of commendation from President Barack Obama.

The FCA students developed a truly original project. As humans begin to explore and inhabit space, they presumed, a time will come to construct buildings for habitation. So they studied the effects of mixing concrete in space in two ways: first by stirring the concrete mixture, and second by vibrating the concrete mixture in solution. They analyzed the molecular structure and integrity of both kinds of concrete using Valley Christian's Atomic Force Microscope. It was an extraordinary partnership—two schools, two hugely different-sized student bodies, and one common denominator: We believe in a limitless God, giving His children a vision beyond themselves for quality education.

The Sky Is Not the Limit

The Quest for Space is only one of the exciting programs administered by the AMSE Institute at Valley Christian Schools. Our students, faculty, and engineers incubate programs for Valley Christian students to share with students in schools everywhere through the Quest Institute for Quality Education.[20] Even fourth-grade elementary students are not too young to participate in the ISS program. All upper elementary students at Valley Christian Elementary School have the privilege to participate on an ISS research team. Students write and transmit their coded solutions to a research experiment via the "Internet of Things"[21] to run on the ISS every school year. Hellyer Elementary School in San Jose, California, and Belleview Elementary School in Sonora, California, were early public school adopters of the Quest for Space ISS program.

It's our deep conviction that every child, regardless of socioeconomic circumstances, should be able to access these kinds of applied math, science, and engineering opportunities. That's why the Quest Institute has helped make these same opportunities available in more than 160 (and counting) schools and organizations across the United States and worldwide since 2011. And engineers continue their development of new and exciting scientific offerings. We'll be hearing more about these thrilling innovations in Chapter Seven.

CHAPTER 4

OVERCOMING
IMPOSSIBLE ODDS

DURING MY CAREER as an educator, all kinds of initiatives to restore quality to our public schools have come and gone. There was New Math in the 1970s, Individualized Instruction and Measurable Objectives in the 1980s, then Project-Based and Outcomes-Based Education (OBE) and the Expected School-wide Learning Results (ESLRs) of the 1990s. More recently we've had No Child Left Behind, Common Core Standards, and Benchmark Assessments. But not one of these was transformative, and none brought quality education for all students. I'm not saying all these programs were total failures, but they focused only on the learning aspects of the Light, Life, and Learning paradigm. As a result, American public education lost its moral compass and rudder.

If you're an educator or a parent who keeps up with educational trends, you're no doubt familiar with the Common Core State Standards. The Common Core State Standards Initiative is a set of college- and career-ready standards for kindergarten through twelfth-grade students in English language arts and mathematics.

Although some states have passed legislation against them, most states have adopted the Common Core Standards.

The goal is to produce high school graduates who are proficient in English and math. But what our schools desperately need in addition to curriculum and academic standards are the Common Virtues so prominent in our nation's founding principles, offering all children a moral foundation for character development. Outstanding teachers and administrators care enough about their students to work tirelessly for higher standards in math, English, and other subjects. Shouldn't they also support a Common Virtues Initiative to help form the values of every student, giving them a moral compass and rudder to discern right from wrong?

The Declaration of Independence affirms that all are created equal. This truth underpins the virtues of mutual respect, honoring the dignity of every person, the value of kindness, honesty, integrity, and treating others the way you would want them to treat you. It's the Golden Rule, and much more. These virtues form the building blocks of good schools, good communities, and good relationships.

I believe a Common Virtues Initiative is the kind of educational movement most Americans would support—and all children deserve—regardless of race, religion, creed, nationality, or ethnicity. While I am a lover of the Bible and read it daily, this initiative would not require official school-led Bible reading and prayer in the public schools. But it would give teachers the opportunity to emphasize character development for their students, promoting good citizenship during every day of the school calendar.

Today we understand more than ever how "the pursuit of happiness" is an empty promise without the opportunity for a quality education. And without the Common Virtues that can offer students a sense of personal dignity, equality, and purpose, quality education will remain out of reach for most children.

PARTNERS IN PURPOSE

Each fall semester, the faculty and staff of Valley Christian Schools make the drive to the Mount Hermon Christian Conference Center, about forty miles southwest of San Jose, for a one-day retreat. It's a time to recharge our batteries and focus on the school's ministry objectives for the coming year. For the 2012 event, I invited Hellyer Elementary principal Jerry Merza and his wife, Lyn, to join us.

On Friday, August 31, a couple of weeks before we were scheduled to head out, I got a phone call from Jerry. He told me Lyn's latest blood test showed the level of her CA-125 cancer marker had plummeted, and when her doctors looked at the latest PET scan results, they declared her cancer free. That was fantastic news. Jerry told me that Lyn's white blood cell count, which had been dangerously low, was now in the normal range. We were thrilled, and we looked forward to both the retreat and the upcoming Hawaii conference.

On September 17, the morning of the retreat, I drove over to Hellyer Elementary to pick up Jerry and Lyn. We had a great conversation as we navigated the winding roads to Mount Hermon. The conference center is in the middle of Sequoia redwood country near the town of Felton, and the weather there is usually beautiful.

I was delighted that Jerry and Lyn were willing to speak to our team. When we gathered together in the auditorium, I told everyone it was a great privilege to be able to introduce the Merzas. Jerry spoke first. He described some of the learning challenges his Hellyer students and teachers were facing, including a large number of students who couldn't learn English from their parents, and many more whose families faced difficult economic circumstances. He expressed special gratitude for the VCS students who had made such an impact on the quality of education at Hellyer by mentoring, encouraging, and befriending the younger pupils.

"Without the programs your students have brought to Hellyer this fall, our students wouldn't have a choir, musical instrument instruction, athletic coaching, art, dance, robotics, or Valley Christian student tutors who help teach and inspire our students to learn. The connections your students make with our students truly inspire them, give them hope, and foster higher achievement. When your students come on campus, it's the most exciting time of the week for our students. Thank you for all you are doing. It's making a significant difference at Hellyer Elementary School."

There was heartfelt applause when Jerry paused, but he continued. "Lyn and I grew up in Catholic homes," he said. "We're thankful for what our parents and the Catholic Church taught us about God, but we strayed from our faith. We didn't talk about our faith to each other or our children. Like most people, we just focused on taking care of the kids and our careers.

"We seldom attended church. You could say we were Christmas and Easter Christians. So when cancer attacked Lyn, we didn't have a solid faith to turn to for encouragement, or strength to face the devastating news. When Dr. Daugherty asked me if we would like a group of Valley Christian students to pray for Lyn's healing, we didn't know how to respond at first. But we eventually decided that prayer was what we needed. We received news about three weeks ago from the doctor that Lyn is cancer free. We can't thank God enough. But I'll let Lyn tell her own story."

At that point, Jerry sat down in the front row, and Lyn rose to speak. "I'm not accustomed to standing in front of people and speaking," she said, "but I wanted to let you know what the children you teach are doing and have done for my family and me. And I wanted to thank you all personally." Looking at her husband, she smiled and said, "What Jerry just said about our church attendance is an exaggeration. We weren't Christmas and Easter Christians;

we were more like wedding and funeral Christians. But things have changed in a big way for our family. Because of your prayers, I'm cancer free now, and I know God is with me." Many faces beamed and nodded back at her.

"When I agreed to go to the elementary school so the Valley students could pray for me," Lyn continued, "I didn't know what to expect. No one had ever prayed for me that way, and honestly, I didn't understand why anyone would want to, let alone a group of high school students. So I was nervous, not knowing what would happen. I brought my three-year-old son, Brayden, and a friend who was visiting from out of town. I expected maybe five or six people to show up, but when I walked into the room it was filled with more than thirty people. I was so surprised. But Dr. Daugherty invited us to sit in the middle of the room, and everyone gathered around us, placing their hands on me while reaching around to each other so we would all be connected. Then they started praying, one person at a time. I was deeply moved. I had never experienced anything like that before. I had never felt so much love around me in that way. It was amazing. So thank you. I'm truly grateful."

When Lyn finished her comments, tears of joy dampened the eyes of almost everyone in the room, including mine. Lyn too brushed back tears of gratitude as she spoke. We all felt Jesus in our midst as we thanked God for everything He was doing for the Hellyer students and Jerry's wonderful family.

MOVED TO ACTION

Following the retreat, Jerry and I met several times to coordinate our keynote address for the conference in Hawaii the following month. Speaking to more than a thousand delegates from all over the world would be a daunting task. We prayed for God's help and a sense of calm to speak comfortably and naturally.

Before we spoke, we featured the short documentary video Ed Silvoso had arranged to film at Hellyer about JULI. Then Lyn and Jerry shared their story of God's goodness in their personal lives and at Hellyer Elementary School. Everyone marveled. The conference in Hawaii was a great inspiration and encouragement for all of us. And my vision enlarged for bringing Light, Life, and Learning to the nation's public schools, with God's goodness, peace, and joy.

Shortly after the conclusion of the keynote message at the Hilton Waikiki Resort, a simple but profound strategy came to mind. My plan was for Jerry to ask Carla Haakma, the principal of Los Arboles Elementary School, if she would like to have the same Junior University and Lighthouse Initiative programs at her school that Jerry enjoyed at Hellyer. Then, if she agreed, I would ask the principal of Andrew Hill High School for help in securing student volunteers from the public high school to join with our Valley Christian High School students as mentors at Los Arboles. The thought ignited my heart, and as soon as Jerry heard the idea, he was on board. When Jerry became enthused, I knew the Supreme Court Judge of the heavens and the earth was once again leading the way.

On our first school day after returning from Hawaii, Jerry called Principal Haakma to ask if she had any interest in bringing the programs to her school. Her answer was a resounding "yes." Not only that, she told him, "We have a sister school, Daniel Lairon Elementary School, and we work side by side with them. It would be great if we can also include them in the programs."

When Jerry gave me the news, I knew we would need a lot more mentors to serve all three elementary schools. Most of the students from those schools would eventually attend Andrew Hill High School, so it seemed like a great match. I made a phone call to Andrew Hill's principal, Bettina Lopez, expecting to work my way through an automated phone tree. But to my surprise, a pleasant voice answered the phone on the first or second ring.

"Hello, I'm Clifford Daugherty, president of Valley Christian Schools," I said. "We have a wonderful community service program for students at Hellyer Elementary School, and now Principal Carla Haakma at Los Arboles Elementary would like to expand the program to her school and Daniel Lairon as well. We've stretched our volunteer students and resources about as far as we can, so I'd like to arrange a meeting with Principal Lopez to ask for help from Andrew Hill High School in enlisting student volunteers to serve alongside our Valley students at Los Arboles and Daniel Lairon schools."

The next words I heard shocked me. "Yes, we can meet. I am Bettina Lopez."

I'm not sure how often Principal Lopez answered the office phones while leading a high school of close to twenty-two hundred students, but I had a distinct impression the Supreme Court Judge of the heavens and the earth had arranged the call. I was encouraged, and I imagined what a wonderful cooperative venture Andrew Hill and Valley Christian might develop.

The events that followed brought to mind the words in the last paragraph of the Declaration of Independence: "with a firm reliance on . . . divine Providence." I became convinced the same divine Providence that founded and established the United States of America in the 18th century is fully capable of restoring Light, Life, and Learning in America's public schools.

When we held our first Junior University planning meeting in my office on Friday, October 19, 2012, the principals of four schools were in attendance, including Carla Haakma from Los Arboles Elementary, Bettina Lopez from Andrew Hill High School, Jerry Merza from Hellyer Elementary, and Mark Lodewyk, principal of

Valley Christian High School. Dr. John Porter, superintendent of the Franklin–McKinley School District, and Maria Dehghanfard, principal of Daniel Lairon Elementary, attended their first planning meeting on November 16.

Over the coming months, we developed the plans and prepared to launch the expanded Junior University and Lighthouse Initiative at Los Arboles and Daniel Lairon schools in the fall of 2013. Volunteer students from Andrew Hill High School would team up with a growing number of Valley Christian High School students as tutors and mentors for the during-school and after-school enrichment activities.

ACROSS ALL BOUNDARIES

On October 22, just two weeks and one day after returning from the Global Transform Our World conference in Hawaii, I looked out my office window to the north to see a brilliant rainbow. It was so magnificent that I grabbed my iPhone and took a picture through the window, hoping to get a nice shot to share with my wife, Kris. The photo turned out remarkably well, and I couldn't help but wonder if the rainbow was a sign from God that He would bless and prosper the plans Jerry Merza and I had brought back from the conference. It seemed too perfect to be a coincidence.

As I studied the photo, a thought began to form in my mind, and a quick look at Google Maps confirmed my hunch. The rainbow formed a canopy directly over Andrew Hill High School and the Franklin–McKinley School District campuses that had joined Junior University and the Lighthouse Initiative. Furthermore, the rainbow touched the earth at Hellyer Elementary School, where the prototype of Junior University began in 2006–2007. Later, after Sylvandale Middle School joined the program, I saw how it too was covered by the rainbow.

The photograph made me think about the various schools and everything involved in launching the programs. While much more could be written about all that took place during our planning sessions throughout the 2012–2013 school year, the leadership team from the various schools worked together enthusiastically to implement Junior University and the Lighthouse Initiative and lay a foundation for expanding the programs even further. Now, as I'm writing and reflect on the rainbow, I can only imagine how far the rainbow reaches.

Our partnership with Andrew Hill High School proved especially fruitful. A strategy emerged to blend the high school mentoring students from both Andrew Hill and Valley Christian to launch the Junior University tutoring program at Lairon Elementary. The Christian Club at Andrew Hill High School volunteered to help start a Kids Club at Lairon that would include both components of the JULI program (Junior University and the Lighthouse Initiative). Since VCS already provided bus transportation for the mentors each week, we agreed to transport the Andrew Hill students as well, without cost to our new friends. Before long, about 265 student trips took place each week to serve the students in our neighborhood public elementary schools.

Working in partnership with our local public school educators was exhilarating. The usual boundaries that often separate people, including economic differences, ethnic characteristics, district lines, public vs. private school distinctions, and religious labels, completely evaporated. Everyone involved understood that every child is precious because, as the Declaration of Independence clearly states, we are all equal in the eyes of our Creator.

This "across all boundaries" cooperation enriched the lives of the participants, as shared resources multiplied the impact of everyone's efforts. Who benefits the most? Undoubtedly, it is the students in every one of our participating schools. The elementary students receive tutoring and support, improving their academic performance, while the high school mentors discover the joy of transforming the hopes and achievements of young children through their volunteer service.

A PASSION FOR LEARNING

One of the most important discoveries we have made through the amazing co-curricular programs developed on our campus and in the public schools has to do with the power of adult volunteers and mentors to help transform students' lives. What we learned is that the most accomplished people in our communities, those who are the most entrepreneurial, and those who have a strategic mind and a can-do attitude are contagious. They easily accomplish extraordinary things to help mold and shape the minds and attitudes of the young people who will become the leaders of the next generation.

In August 2015, I received a call from Erich Shaffer, who heads a team of 170 engineers at Cisco Systems in Silicon Valley. Mr. Shaffer wanted to set up a meeting. "I'm intrigued by what you're doing at your school," he told me, "and I think I should help in some way." Cisco, as any tech savvy person knows, is one of the world's leading IT firms and networking giants. So when Erich came to the Skyway campus to learn about our Applied Math, Science, and Engineering programs, we were thrilled.

During a follow-up discussion, I told Erich about Valley's new partnership with the Firehouse Community Development Corporation to launch the ISS program at Andrew Hill High School. Pastor Sonny Lara heads the Firehouse, and it's an incredible outreach to at-risk students. To be accepted into the Firehouse program, students must have at least four F's. For the most part, these young people have little or no interest in school and are in danger of becoming high school dropouts. Erich enthusiastically agreed to mentor these at-risk Andrew Hill High School students to build and place science experiments aboard the International Space Station. Pastor Sonny, Erich, and I believed that even the most at-risk students could thrive when challenged and given the opportunity to achieve the seemingly impossible.

Danny Kim, who serves as chief technology officer at the Quest Institute for Quality Education, met with the Firehouse students and explained how the Quest for Space program works. If the students showed interest and accepted the challenge, they could achieve something very few people in the world have accomplished. It's the sort of program that could put them on a pathway toward university acceptance and a professional career. For most of these students, they would be the first in their families to attend college. (You'll hear more about this story from Danny's perspective in Chapter Eight.)

Erich and other adult mentors gave this initiative their full support. Before long, Erich was coaching two teams of students who signed up for the program. Troubled teens whom some people had written off as hopeless began impressing everyone with their dedication and hard work. And it wasn't long before we all had a pleasant surprise. When some of the high achievers at Andrew Hill saw what was going on with the Firehouse students, they felt slighted and wanted the same opportunity.

When Pastor Lara told me about it, I was delighted. At that point, I contacted Andrew Hill's new principal, Jose Hernandez, and he opened the door for the high-achieving students to participate as well. The ISS program is fun but demanding. The fear that the more advanced students would outshine and intimidate the at-risk students, however, proved unfounded. When given the opportunity, every student succeeded.

Erich Shaffer's strategic thinking and "get it done" mindset was contagious. His way of thinking and organizing and his presence infected all of the students with hope and a new passion for learning. Their view of themselves and their perspectives about their future possibilities became completely transformed. Every one of those at-risk students, who had rarely earned a grade higher than F, turned a major corner. They began working harder, achieving better grades in all subjects, setting new academic goals, and discussing new aspirations to go on to college after high school graduation.

The passion, dedication, and amazing achievements of the students prompted Erich to make an astounding pledge at the end-of-the-year awards ceremony. With parents and friends present, he offered every one of his mentees a job as a Cisco engineer upon completing college with an engineering degree. Who would have thought such a thing possible? These were young people with little in their future besides the prospect of poverty and hardship. But they were transformed, and their view of themselves and their future goals completely changed. All it took was exposure to mentors who cared about them, who had an infectious passion for showing young people how to "get it done."

These kinds of applied learning opportunities ignite the interest of students in their core academic courses. An insatiable thirst for knowledge takes hold, and a passionate appreciation for the wonderful work of certified teachers comes to life. Volunteer mentors can spur these young people—who are often just like themselves at that age—to visualize and believe that a great professional future is within reach.

INSPIRATIONAL ROLE MODELS

Mentors are necessary for every school, and that's why we must challenge the most successful professionals from every community to get on board. Many community leaders seem to have the idea, "I'm not qualified to teach young people. The people who are best qualified to teach and inspire school kids have teaching credentials, and I don't have one." It's a common misconception, but it's not true. Professionals know what it took to build their careers, and the students set similar goals for themselves with the encouragement of their volunteer mentors.

Think about it for a moment. People who spend their college years training to become certified teachers prepare themselves to teach specific subject matter, critical analysis, and some types of application to their students. Meanwhile, entrepreneurs, engineers, artists, government leaders, scientists, and medical professionals also acquire specialized skills. What they've learned in their careers gives them the resources to be especially powerful mentors.

For example, a concert pianist doesn't need a teaching credential. But a concert pianist would likely be among the most powerful influences for a talented young person who desires to discover and develop his or her God-given musical talent. A student who otherwise might never have an opportunity for a weekly piano lesson at that level would be transformed and energized. The same is true for all professions. To transform American education, we need to abolish the myth that unless you have a teaching credential, you're not qualified to mentor and inspire a child.

At first, Erich Shaffer thought he didn't have the proper training to instruct at-risk high school students. He loved the program, and he knew he could help young people develop an experiment to fly on the International Space Station. But he had to be convinced. The magic happened when the students with four or more F's dared to attempt an "impossible" project, one that became possible because Erich Shaffer committed two hours every Wednesday after school to help the students succeed. Erich infected them with a new passion for learning and achievement. Their grades dramatically improved, and they set new goals. Every one of them made plans to attend college. Many decided they wanted to become engineers at Cisco.

Of course, mentors can't replace quality teachers. Certified teachers, as subject-matter experts trained in educational principles, are essential to teaching students needed skills in preparation for their emerging careers. But every child can also benefit tremendously from exposure to the most successful math, science, and engineering entrepreneurs in their communities, as well as business professionals, artists, and other skilled specialists. I discovered through experience that quality education is most easily within reach of students who have the benefit of extraordinary teachers as well as the applied learning made possible by mentors with experience scaling their professional ladders.

George Sousa is an excellent example. George's career as a physicist with General Electric took him all over the world building nuclear power plants. About the time he retired, he heard of Valley Christian Schools' amazing International Space Station (ISS) science experiments project. His curiosity compelled him to check it out, and he offered to help some students who were struggling with their ISS projects. Before long, George started showing up at the school on a regular basis as a volunteer mentor, asking the right questions and helping students find the right answers.

George doesn't have a teaching credential, but he has a whole career of solving what most people would imagine to be complex problems and achieving seemingly unachievable goals. That's a way of thinking that can inspire children in every American school. Sadly, however, the impact and influence of experienced pros like George Sousa are absent in most schools. Most schools haven't considered how valuable these kinds of programs can be with the input of seasoned professionals.

I'm still astonished at the way it all happened. Some of George's mentee students said they wanted to become aeronautical engineers, so they asked George if they could build a rocket after school as a co-curricular project. Because George has a "can do" attitude and an "anything is possible" strategic mindset, he said, "Sure, if you'll commit to the work after school, you can build a rocket." The students agreed and got to work. They designed and built every part of that seventeen-foot, multi-stage rocket. George took the mentoring challenge, and the students became mesmerized with all they learned and accomplished. They listened, learned, and worked together at every meeting until they launched their rocket for multiple flights.

We have remarkable math and science teachers at Valley Christian Schools, but not one of them had the experience to help their students build a rocket. On the other hand, without our wonderful certified math teachers in the core academic courses, the students would not have had the math skills needed to build a rocket. But they certainly took their math and science courses more seriously after they began their rocket building. George's story ought to repeat thousands of times in our American high schools.

The JULI model provides an important foundation of the Quest for Quality Education in all sorts of schools, with the mentoring influence of some of the most successful professionals in every community as a vital component. We want the professional achievers in every community to know they have something special to offer the children in their neighborhood schools. Their hard-won professional knowledge and expertise are priceless.

THE POWER OF ONE: "SINK THE *BISMARCK*!"

Maybe you know the story of the German battleship *Bismarck*. It's not as well known today as it was a generation or two ago, but the story took place during the Second World War and had a profound impact on the war's outcome. It's also a historical event with an important message for us today, since we're in a huge war as well—a war for the hearts and minds of our children and the next generation.

The *Bismarck* was the crown jewel of the German navy. It boasted the latest and greatest technology, and the proud commanders of the Nazi fleet believed their great battleship was unsinkable. Sailors assigned to the *Bismarck* scoffed at any hint of weakness or vulnerability. Yet, within a forty-eight-hour sequence of events in 1941, most of them would be dead—entombed within the broken and twisted hull of the sunken vessel, sixteen thousand feet below the surface of the North Atlantic Ocean.

As the pride of Hitler's naval forces, the heavily armored *Bismarck* was a beast on the seas—an 823-foot tiger displacing 50,300 tons, ready to pounce on her prey as she prowled the northern sea lanes. She saw action for only eight months but struck fear into the hearts of Allied commanders as a killer of their vitally important supply ships.

It was with some excitement, then, when the British naval vessels *HMS Hood* and *HMS Prince of Wales* intercepted the *Bismarck* in the narrow strait between Iceland and Greenland on the morning of May 24, 1941. On that cold spring day, the three warships went head-to-head in the Battle of the Denmark Strait.

The *HMS Hood*, though the flagship of the Royal Fleet, was wholly inferior to the battleship built by the Nazi engineers. The vast superiority of the *Bismarck* proved to be the *Hood*'s doom. Ten minutes into the battle, the *Hood* exploded into flames, and in barely three minutes sank to a watery grave. Of the fourteen hundred British sailors on board, only three survived.

The main deck of the *Bismarck* erupted in cheers as the *Hood* slipped beneath the frigid waves. The *Prince of Wales*, having sustained heavy damage, made a hasty tactical retreat. But when news of the disaster reached the headquarters of British Prime Minister Winston Churchill, his order was immediately broadcast to the entire British feet: "Sink the *Bismarck!*"

"I don't care how you do it," Churchill erupted. "You must sink the *Bismarck!*"

On his command, sixteen British warships scrambled into action, descending upon the *Bismarck*'s last known position south of Greenland. British commanders ordered the fleet to hunt the *Bismarck* down, even if it meant running out of fuel and exposing themselves to enemy fire.

It was a formidable task. But finally, three of the British vessels cornered their enemy three hundred miles off the Irish coast. With his position compromised, German Admiral Johann Lütjens ordered the *Bismarck* to make a sweeping circular maneuver behind her pursuers—a brilliant tactic that allowed the Nazi vessel to slip away undetected. Then the *Bismarck* made a run for occupied France, and it looked as if she would reach safe harbor with the protection of the German Air Force.

On the morning of May 26, however, a British reconnaissance aircraft spotted the *Bismarck*. Though the bulk of Britain's naval vessels still lagged far behind the German battleship, the aircraft carrier *Ark Royal* was in the vicinity. Her arsenal included a squadron of Swordfish biplanes, an open cockpit aircraft resembling those of World War One vintage, with a top speed of barely 125 miles per hour and a payload consisting of a single torpedo.

Late in the day, fifteen Swordfish launched from the *Ark Royal* during a heavy storm. The biplanes descended on the *Bismarck* like a cloud of mosquitoes attempting to penetrate an elephant's thick hide. One German officer said later, "It was incredible to see such obsolete-looking planes having the nerve to attack a fire-spitting mountain like the *Bismarck*."[22]

Most of the torpedoes fired from the Swordfish missed the *Bismarck*, but two hit their mark. One exploded harmlessly against the ship's thick hull, while the second struck near the port rudder shaft. It was an unlikely shot, hitting the *Bismarck* at her weakest point—the rudders of her steering mechanism. The blast did not destroy the rudder but jammed it into a locked twelve-degree turn. Unbelievably, the tiny "mosquito" forced the *Bismarck* to steam in circles, helplessly awaiting an attack by the British fleet.

"What nobody talks about were the conditions—they were unbelievable," recalled pilot John Moffat, speaking in the spring of 2009.[23] Then age eighty-nine, he had recently written a book, *I Sank the Bismarck*, about his experiences that day in 1941. Moffat was one of the fifteen Swordfish pilots who took off from the aircraft carrier *Ark Royal* on their attack mission.

"The ship was pitching sixty feet, water was running over the decks, and the wind was blowing at seventy or eighty miles per hour. And nobody mentions the deck hands who had to bring the planes up from the hangars—they did something special. After they brought them up, they had to open the wings, which took ten men for each wing. And then they had to wind a handle to get the starters working. . . . After take-off we climbed to six thousand feet to get above the really thick cloud, and we knew when we were near because all hell broke loose with *Bismarck*'s fire. We got the order to attack, and I went down and saw the enormous bloody ship. I thought the *Ark Royal* was big, but this one, blimey.

"I must have been under two thousand yards when I was about to launch the torpedo at the bow, but as I was about to press the button, I heard in my ear 'not now, not now.'

"I turned around and saw the navigator leaning right out of the plane with his backside in the air. Then I realized what he was doing—he was looking at the sea because if I had let the torpedo go and it had hit a wave, it could have gone anywhere. I had to put it in a trough.

"Then I heard him say 'let it go,' and I pressed the button. Then I heard him say 'we've got a runner'—and I got out of there."

The term "runner" means a torpedo that would run clear to its target without bouncing off a wave. Moffat pulled up before the torpedo hit and didn't see it strike.

One day later, with the *Bismarck* unable to maneuver, four British warships pummeled the German vessel with more than twenty-eight hundred shells, scoring four hundred hits. After a withering ninety-minute assault, the *Bismarck* lay dead in the water, with fires breaking out, water penetrating the decks, and many lives lost.

The battleship's upper works were almost destroyed, but her engines still functioned. German survivor Hans Zimmermann confirmed later that salt water had penetrated the boilers. Fearing an explosion, the engineers reduced speed to seven knots. Rather than risk the ship's capture, the First Officer gave the order to abandon ship, and German-rigged scuttling explosives did what more than four hundred British shells could not. At 10:40 a.m., the *Bismarck* disappeared below the ocean's surface. Of the twenty-two hundred crew members on board, only 115 survived.

CONNECTING THE DOTS

What a David and Goliath story! Just one brave pilot, John Moffat, and his one navigator, John "Dusty" Miller, sealed the fate of Germany's fiercest warship. They turned the tide of battle from the likely escape of the formidable *Bismarck* to a crucial victory, a milestone in winning the war.

The German *Bismarck* was Europe's greatest naval warship, built to strengthen Hitler's Third Reich as the Nazi war machine threatened world domination and tyranny. But by the grace of God, just one antiquated biplane, piloted by just one man, with one navigator and only a single torpedo managed to secure the doom of the great hulking beast, the *Bismarck*, sending it to the ocean floor.

Think of it. A single, tiny, obsolete-looking Swordfish biplane, armed with just one torpedo, only one courageous pilot, and his one navigator!

I'm impressed by this story because for our purposes it offers two important lessons. It exemplifies:

1. "The Power of One" principle, and

2. The importance of a fully functioning moral compass and rudder.

If you are the first to volunteer to serve in your neighborhood school as a mentor, or among the first to affirm the Common Virtues in our nation's schools, you might feel weak in the face of our massive public school challenges. Initially, you are likely to feel that the possibilities of making a difference seem hopeless. And in the beginning, your one voice may seem feeble. But remain determined and faithful to fight the good fight as David fought Goliath, and as pilot John Moffat with his navigator attacked the *Bismarck*. Don't lose heart or courage. Remain steadfast and determined, because standing with truth and justice makes the weakest mortal a triumphant warrior. "If God is for us, who can be against us?"[24]

Significantly, John Moffat did not learn until the year 2000 that it was his successful torpedo attack that crippled the *Bismarck*. What an example: We should all be so selfless in our commitment to serve the children of our nation, regardless of whether we have any assurance of recognition for faithful service or even living long enough to see the fruit of our labors. We should have confidence that the Supreme Court Judge of the heavens and the earth will reward the faithfulness of all who help restore Common Virtues, goodness, peace, and joy, and the wonderful educational opportunities we must ensure for the children in our schools.

The rudder of our founding values, embedded in the Declaration of Independence, must be safely reconnected to our nation's schools. We must firmly "hold" and teach the same unchanging, "self-evident" truths to all children in our communities.

The crew of the crippled *Bismarck* tried desperately to repair the ship's damaged rudder but failed. When I made the connection between the fate of that ship and the educational problems facing America today, I began to wonder if our public schools face a similar destiny. Is the rudder of the American education system irreparably damaged?

The lesson we learn from Churchill, the Royal Navy, and pilot John Moffat is captured in Churchill's words on another occasion later that same year: "[N]ever give in, never give in, never, never, never—in nothing, great or small, large or petty—never give in except to convictions of honour and good sense. Never yield to force; never yield to the apparently overwhelming might of the enemy."[25]

To those memorable words I would add: Never give up in defense of truth and the fight for freedom, regardless of the odds. Truth is on the side of freedom, and those who place their faith in the truth will ultimately prevail. That is as true in education as it is in wartime. The seemingly insoluble problems in our public schools are not as insurmountable as some may believe. The same commitment to truth that gave birth to this nation can bring forth a rebirth of quality education in our schools. How quickly and dramatically the circumstances of our public schools could improve!

The *Bismarck* story is rich with analogies and metaphors. A damaged rudder renders America's educational system as dysfunctional. Once the finest in the world, with the noble purpose of extending knowledge and educational opportunity to all, our public education system today is in jeopardy of catastrophic failure. Having lost our rudder, we're turning in circles, waiting for disaster to strike.

Abundant evidence of our predicament confronts us. For example, the Organisation for Economic Co-operation and Development (OECD) publishes the Program for International Student Assessment (PISA), a triennial survey of fifteen-year-old students. The 2015 results show the United States ranked 25th in science, not significantly different from the mean average score among seventy-two participating countries, and tied for 39th in mathematics, significantly below the average.[26] Perhaps most perplexing, an article in *U.S. News & World Report* stated that "American 12th graders were near the bottom of students from 20 nations assessed in advanced math and physics."[27]

At times we may feel like "mosquitoes attempting to penetrate an elephant's thick hide." But we must—for the sake of our children, our families, and our nation—be resolute in the face of our behemoth challenge. Futility is not something we can accept. We ought to be producing future leaders in every profession of influence. We have the capacity and the know-how to achieve that goal. The objective now is to connect the dots and come to grips with what the data are telling us. The story of John Moffat and the *Bismarck* illustrates the principle of "The Power of One."

BE THE ONE!

CHAPTER 5

JULI and the Common
Virtues Initiative

"WHAT MAKES A PUBLIC SCHOOL wary of support
or help from outside groups is that these organizations often come
with an agenda. They have a program they want to introduce, and no
school wants to be co-opted by outsiders."

Jerry Merza was speaking from the heart about his years as principal of Hellyer Elementary School in San Jose, California. Most if
not all public school educators would identify with this perspective.
We described in Chapter Three how the Junior University mentoring
program began. In this chapter, Jerry offers deeper insights as to
how and why he and his public school staff decided Junior University
and Lighthouse Initiative (JULI) programs would be great for their
students.

"What is so beneficial about the partnership with Valley is that
their approach is simply, 'What do you need?' and 'How can we help?'
Not, 'Here's what we're here to give you.'

"That non-threatening approach gave us an opportunity to take a closer look at those programs. After getting to see them in action, the teachers agreed that JULI was what we needed. And for a school that had so many needs, we were able to consider what would be most beneficial for us." Jerry described how he and his staff took the opportunity to brainstorm: "What can we give our students that they really need and don't already have and that the research shows will help them achieve at higher levels?"

This exercise proved enlightening. "Public schools are limited in the resources they have to provide intervention, extra time, or individual attention. In a class of thirty-two," Jerry explained, "the teacher will be dealing with a whole range of achievement levels, from high achievers to those who may be in the fifth grade but reading at a first-grade level. Imagine yourself in a classroom alone with twenty-five to thirty-five children. It is impossible for anyone to connect with every one of them and meet all of their wide-ranging academic and emotional needs. We think we can't make a difference because we don't know how to solve such big problems.

"So the question becomes: 'What is the best way to utilize scarce resources and acquire added resources to meet the needs of all the children in our schools?'

"Our local public schools do a great job helping students at the low end," he went on. "Most of the money poured into the schools tends to support the students with academic, social, or behavioral problems. Meanwhile, those at the high end get the least attention. We are secure in thinking these kids are going to achieve no matter what, so we usually turn our focus to the children who are one or two years below grade level and could go either way."

"The JULI programs turned around this approach. When the Valley junior and senior high students came during the school day, they met with our kids, made friends with them, and provided individual tutoring for the at-risk kids and added electives with enriched mentoring opportunities for the average and gifted students. The first year we saw a tremendous increase in achievement for the entire school—in just one year!"

At that time (as described earlier), California measured success for the public schools based on their API scores, with the expectation that every school in the state would reach 800 or above. That was the acceptable threshold. "Two years before I started at Hellyer," Jerry continued, "the school's API was 736, and the district was giving the school a lot of pressure about that. But during my first year as principal, and Hellyer's third full year with Junior University, we climbed to 808, which was fantastic. The improvement was due in large part to the resources of personal time given by the Valley Christian students. More money in our budget wouldn't have produced the same academic results.

"When Junior University was first introduced at Hellyer, before I arrived, it was mainly a tutoring program by Valley students. They gave the elementary school kids someone to look up to—role models the students could aspire to and emulate. The Valley high school students would soon be graduating and going off to top-flight universities, and they were all academically successful. That helped, and it propelled us. We began to dream about additional instructional opportunities: *How else can we use these great students who are about to go to university to help support our kids academically?*"

Jerry continued, "That's when we added the SAM Club and began offering the full JULI program. The mentors and mentees formed positive relationships, and the results were impressive by any standard. And from Valley's perspective, they enjoyed a nice residual effect, because that kind of success gave the high school mentors a sense of confidence, realizing they could be a positive influence in the lives of our kids at Hellyer."

IN THEIR OWN WORDS

It was great for me to hear Jerry's reactions to the JULI approach. What better endorsement than to see how the faculty themselves received the program. Later, when Jerry and I had the opportunity to interact with a couple of sixteen-year-old juniors on our campus who had come up through the Lighthouse Initiative at Hellyer, I got a firsthand look at how two of Jerry's former students responded to the program.

These young women had signed up for the JULI programs in fourth grade and now had earned scholarships to attend Valley Christian High School. What had excited them most about JULI, they told me, was the opportunity to learn a musical instrument. They received weekly music lessons from Valley Christian mentors, and they were trusted to take the instruments home to practice.

"Mrs. Nardi, the Lighthouse director, said we could learn about all kinds of instruments," Amy told me, "and I thought, *Wow! I always wanted to learn how to play an instrument. That would be so cool.* My parents couldn't afford to pay for private lessons, but the Lighthouse lessons were free. So I went home and said, 'Mom, you've got to sign this permission slip because it's going to be so cool.'"

During her first year in Lighthouse, Amy studied saxophone and percussion. She also played sports for a while. The kids in her group played soccer, basketball, and other activities, but Amy said she preferred the music lessons. She even gave up sports to add clarinet and piano lessons to her repertoire.

Amy's best friend, Victoria, told me the Lighthouse Initiative gave her options for trying new things, and she discovered she loved the arts program. She was accepted into Valley's Conservatory of the Arts when she arrived at our high school, studying music and photography.

"The JULI programs influenced my perception of the various disciplines in the conservatory," Victoria said, "and helped me understand how I can apply myself. Before that, I didn't think of myself as a creative person. I was always studying, and I thought that's all I could ever do."

JULI turned on the lights for both girls. "The Lighthouse gave me a creative outlet I didn't know I had," Victoria told me. "I'm in the science programs now, and my goal is to become a doctor. I have other interests, though, so I might want to be a wedding planner or a photographer. Or maybe I'll be a doctor and do photography on the side." Both Amy and Victoria discovered a whole new range of options.

"I always looked forward to Lighthouse," Amy recalled. "I had only one good friend in elementary school, and I felt secluded and isolated. Lighthouse gave me an opportunity to expand my horizons and dabble in new things. For the first time, I was able to express myself. When the Valley students came down to Hellyer, they were accepting of who we were. They made us feel welcome and appreciated, and that was a comfortable place to be in."

Like her friend Victoria, Amy also realized she had the opportunity to give back. "This was the first time I experienced people giving back to the community, and that triggered me," she said. "I told myself, 'One day I'm going to go to Valley, join the class, and become a mentor myself so I can give back to my community.'" And that's just what she did. Both Victoria and Amy began serving as mentors to the students in three of our local elementary schools. Amy told me her goal is to get her college degree and come back to Valley one day as a teacher.

I'm always impressed when I have the opportunity to chat with Valley students. They're so bright and energetic. High-achieving students like Amy and Victoria remind me that the future of this nation and our ability to compete in an expanding global marketplace can become bright. They are innovative, creative, ambitious, and compassionate. They're going to be the ones who create companies and bring innovation and opportunity to others.

What leaped out at me after my conversation with Amy and Victoria was the importance of investing in bright students like these two young women. The fact is, for decades now, too many schools have not invested the needed resources for challenging our nation's most capable students. Schools expect higher performing students to be already self-motivated, and figure they're going to do well even without attention.

But all of the children in our community schools need and deserve the same opportunities. Through JULI and cooperative programs like the Firehouse initiative, student mentors and local professionals can have a powerful and transforming influence on students in all of our neighborhood schools.

ENABLING ACHIEVERS

The story of the ISS program with the Firehouse students at Andrew Hill High School in the previous chapter shows how even the lowest achieving students can rise to new heights when challenged by someone who believes in them. So what is it that supports a gifted student, one who gets good grades but is likely bored at school or certainly not excited about it? Almost all gifted and inspired achievers have someone they look up to, someone telling them, "You're amazing! I know you can do it. I believe in you, and I believe you can do great things." That's what great mentors communicate with their mentees. They give children the courage to attempt great things, permission to fail, and the courage to keep on trying, no matter what. And when mentors and teachers partner together to offer applied learning projects, learning explodes.

Yes, quality teachers are essential, but the benefit of great teachers is often lost when students don't have the opportunity to discover and express their innate, God-given talents in harmony with their passions. For these students, a passion for learning most often is also lost. That's where mentors from the community make such a huge difference.

If students are "wired" by the Creator as runners, but they're not able to run in sporting programs like track and field, they're not likely to realize their academic potential either, because they're frustrated. What gives them the emotional energy needed to learn academically is the freedom to exercise their giftedness, passion, and joy as they run. Likewise, if kids are passionate about the arts or science but don't have an outlet for those interests, they're going to be bored and won't enjoy going to school every day. They're not inspired; they haven't come alive to learning because their innate gifts and passions are frustrated.

The discovery of this truth at Hellyer led to the origin of the Lighthouse Initiative programs. Jerry Merza wanted to see how his school could stimulate more of its students to perform at higher academic levels, and he believed enrichment opportunities would pay dividends. That's when he and Cindy Nardi developed the SAM Club, to bring Valley Christian students accomplished in sports, the arts, or music to mentor the public school kids in all of these areas.

In addition to leading the after-school SAM Club activities, Valley student mentors—primarily athletes, artists, dancers, and musicians—worked with kids during the school day who were enrolled in the program by their teachers. Varsity athletes taught the younger kids how to play team sports, breaking down the rules for each sport and teaching the individual skills. They weren't just playing games but teaching children the fundamentals of the sport. Meanwhile, the art tutors worked with students in one or more of the arts programs, helping them to discover their gifts and passion for art, music, dance, cheer, and other disciplines.

As Jerry pointed out, "It's hard for adults to sit and listen to lectures for six or seven hours a day, so how can we expect elementary school children to do that? Giving them an outlet to exercise their bodies as well as their minds was very academically productive."

With the JULI programs, students who wanted to dance learned to dance, while others learned art or drama or took musical instrument lessons. We at VCS wanted their principal and the teachers to make all the educational decisions, but students had a say in which activities would be available. Some were eager to learn modern dance while others favored something more traditional, so their preferences shaped the programs their mentors offered. The mentors met with the public school students and talked it out, and together they came up with something everyone liked. The goal was to give the students ownership of the program. That approach proved so popular that the strategy has continued with great success ever since it started in 2012.

We share these examples for our readers to imagine how they might connect with students as mentors.

MAKING IT WORK IN THE SCHOOL

Jerry explained the viewpoint of the administration and faculty at Hellyer Elementary School from his inside angle as principal. Looking back at the success of the JULI program, he said, "At first a few teachers were hesitant to give up their instructional minutes. Especially the upper-grade teachers didn't see the importance of this program. They thought they were giving up academic time so the kids could play. Achievement scores of their students determine teacher evaluations and influence their salaries. So some of the teachers felt the SAM Club program was too risky and decided not to get involved in the beginning.

"But several others recognized its significance. They understood that mentoring in sports, arts, and music and in all the other activities their students cared about was important because it helped their students feel more appreciated and fulfilled. These enrichment opportunities fueled their emotional gas tanks, so they were ready and willing to learn.

"One of the key success factors for Hellyer involves the role of the school's resource coordinator, Liz Nandakumar. Because of her job, Liz has a little more flexibility in her schedule, and she is a big supporter of the JULI programs. She was instrumental in helping start the mentoring program. As a boots-on-the-ground person at Hellyer, she coordinates all the JULI activities. That's important in a program like this, because there's so much happening.

"When they're properly trained, resource teachers are among a school's greatest assets. They not only serve students with disabilities and special needs; they're also trained to serve exceptionally high achieving children with great potential. We were thrilled to discover a strategy to help enable all of our neighborhood students to pursue their Quests for Excellence.

"I don't think we would have had the success we experienced without the support of people like Liz. It's a challenge to introduce pull-out-of-class programs for student activities such as choir, instrumental music, science, or whatever. Some of the teachers in the elementary schools would say, 'Shut the door and stay out of here. I've got a job to do.' We certainly understand that attitude. That's the passion of a dedicated teacher. They often feel there is never enough time in the day to do their job, and here was another program to take their kids out of class.

"But once these programs were underway, I think the teachers became as enthusiastic as the students. When students can get involved in activities that line up with their God-given talents, they feel empowered to fulfill their purpose and their destiny—what they're on this Earth to do. They begin discovering who they were made to be. And they almost always go back to their regular classes with a much better attitude and an excitement to learn."

The advantages of a comprehensive education extend on many levels. The self-esteem movement says that if students believe in themselves, they'll be okay. But the JULI model says, "Here's *why* you should believe in yourself." The programs help develop the skills and interests that will allow students to find their purpose in life. Instead of some sort of artificial self-esteem, they give the children healthy self-respect through skill development and achievement, with a new appreciation for what they have to contribute to others.

In the effort to remediate low student achievement at the junior high level, many of our public schools decided to get rid of all electives, except physical education since it's a state requirement. So the schools doubled up on English and math, made sure the students had P.E., and that was it.

So what happened? The API scores of those schools declined even more. The school strategists had inadvertently removed intrinsic motivation and emotional support by eliminating almost all of the enrichment activities for their students. Since students no longer had a sense of anticipation and enjoyment, suspension rates and gang activity dramatically increased.

When schools don't offer the engaging activities students look forward to, student achievement fades dramatically, with the inevitable loss of readiness for learning. Our objectives were different. We wanted the kids to wake up in the morning eager to get to school, thinking, *I can't wait to go to my guitar class or my choir class.* If they knew they could participate in activities they truly enjoyed, they were much more likely to be emotionally prepared to learn in their math, English, science, and other core academic studies. That's one reason why we strive for comprehensive educational offerings.

Jerry Merza continues the story from his perspective as principal of Hellyer Elementary School.

THE BENEFITS OF INTEGRATING COMMON VIRTUES

"Of course, we weren't able to rely on Christian faith during the school day at the local public schools, but we needed a moral authority we could agree on to teach good character and instill a culture of goodness, peace, and joy. We acknowledged the value of the A^3 strategy of Academic Achievement, Artistic Beauty, and Athletic Distinction, and wanted these programs to stand on a solid moral foundation.

"We realized that the profound wording of the preamble to the Declaration of Independence would serve very well as a solid moral authority we could all affirm. In place of the Bible and the teachings of Jesus, the transcendent words of the Declaration can serve perfectly for any school.

"At Hellyer, we started emphasizing the Common Virtues as a legacy of the nation's founding document. They were incorporated as the teachers interacted with the students and as the students interacted with each other. We set the bar high and taught the children to treat each other with respect. The entire staff began infusing Common Virtues into everything we did at the school. We called it our character development program, and made it clear that this is our culture at Hellyer.

"Before we started doing the SAM Clubs, mentoring the students in sports, arts, and music, there were many problems with student behavior on campus. The symptoms included students wearing gang colors and other negative gang influences. We had high student absences, fighting among students, school suspensions, and other problems.

"One time the police came to confiscate the contraband when students brought beer onto the campus. They tried to hide it in a trash container in the boys' bathroom. Another group of kids even started a fire in the bathroom, and we were thankful they didn't burn down the school. These were ten-, eleven-, and twelve-year-old kids! We had an officer assigned to the school, and a community liaison from the police department from time to time. But funding for that program was minimal, and it was often difficult to get an officer on campus in a real emergency. Graffiti posed a constant problem. But this was the environment from day one, and many of the local schools had similar issues.

"It took a couple of years to percolate up through the system, but we began seeing, especially in the fifth and sixth grades, how suspensions, fights, and gang activity started to wane as we implemented the Junior University program with the Common Virtues. Over time, graffiti almost completely disappeared. We could see the benefits, especially after we integrated Christian faith into many of the enrichment activities with parent permission during the after-school Lighthouse Initiative. That's when we saw these efforts beginning to transform the entire school.

"In 2013, at the beginning of the second year of the full JULI program, Cindy Nardi and I were talking one day, and I asked her, 'How many students do you think we'll have in the after-school Lighthouse Initiative?' The Lighthouse Initiative includes Bible lessons, prayer, and many enrichment activities. Cindy said we might have as many as seventy. So I told her, 'Okay, I'll have seventy permission forms ready for the students to take home to their parents.' I thought that was a pretty big number if all those forms came back signed. Then when the first day came, I asked Cindy, 'How many kids did you have today?' She told me all seventy students with signed permission forms had attended the program, and at least sixty more were interested and had asked for forms! That spoke volumes to me. The kids knew about the program from the previous year. They knew the components—it's a faith-based program—and that's what was drawing them to it.

"At Hellyer, the student body is about seventy percent Hispanic and thirty percent Vietnamese. The Vietnamese children come mainly from Buddhist families, so for them to embrace Christian principles in this way was remarkable. We saw the entire school transformed, especially in the way the students treated each other. The first year I had all these discipline problems in the office—my 'frequent fliers' I called them, because they consistently repeated as offenders. But after we launched the Lighthouse Initiative, I didn't see those kids nearly as often, and some of them dramatically changed. I didn't have to see them in my office at all anymore.

"It doesn't require a lot of imagination to see what could happen if these programs disseminate throughout the public school system. Of course, there isn't a Valley Christian Schools in most communities. But Christians attend churches in just about every community. We like to have volunteers from the community, and local churches are places with people who are among the most likely to help.

"We had a church right down the street that asked how they could support the school, and we were so happy to get those resources. We wanted the volunteers to feel they were supporting our school, and we made them feel welcome. In return, they prepared lunches for our teachers every year, which was great. Then they offered to start a homework club, where some volunteers came in to help the kids with their studies. That's a slightly different approach from the Valley model. In that case, the church came with a plan, whereas the Valley volunteers simply ask, 'What do you need?' or 'How can we help?' But school resources are always scarce, and organizations that truly want to help shouldn't hesitate to approach their neighborhood schools about how they can make a meaningful contribution."

A MODEL OF TRANSFORMATION

Jerry Merza's perspective gives insight into the way a Common Virtues Initiative can work in any school. I wouldn't doubt that in some places there might be resistance to the programs we've developed. But if the individuals who object could see the fundamental changes taking place in these tough schools, located in Silicon Valley, they would understand that transformation can happen anywhere. Even the most troubled schools can become models of good citizenship and cooperation when volunteer mentors provide opportunities for children to use their innate talents and gifts, with mentoring opportunities to succeed.

Research has found that a personal and caring relationship between mentor and mentee is a key ingredient to student success. Willem Kooyker and David Shapiro, board chair and president/CEO respectively of a group called MENTOR, summarized the powerful effects of mentoring: "The research base is strong, the need is clear, and the field is ready. We know now, more than ever, that we can meet many needs of young people through the support of caring adults and continued collaborative efforts of schools, businesses, community organizations, government, philanthropy, and young people themselves. Now, with this national survey, young people's powerful voices can help ensure the fate of America and its next generation are not left to chance."[28]

The person who volunteers to teach a child how to play the

trumpet may not be the best trumpet player in the world, but the fact that he or she has taken a personal interest in the child makes that young person believe, *Gosh, I must be somebody. Someone older and more experienced than I am believes I have potential.* That's a very important and transformative realization.

Jerry Merza told me, "We have students in our schools with older siblings, but their brothers and sisters don't pay attention to them. There are also many kids whose parents work all day, and by the time they come home, exhausted and burned out, they don't have the time or inclination to talk to their children." It's hard to imagine how lonely some of these children must be. They feel deserted, which is one of the biggest reasons some decide to join gangs because their gangs provide the only sense of community and belonging they've ever had. One of the beautiful aspects of the Valley program is the way the junior and senior high mentors take an interest in these kids, build a relationship with them, and make them laugh. That makes such a difference.

Jerry added, "Providing volunteer mentors for the kids involved in elementary enrichment courses also strengthens the feeder system for the local junior high schools. That's why Principal Dan Fowler at Sylvandale Junior High, in our community, told me he loves the JULI approach. For example, from an administrator's point of view, every junior high school needs a music program and some sort of band. But it's very difficult to launch a band in junior high when the elementary schools don't have the resources to offer an instrumental music program to their students. If the kids coming up from the elementary schools don't have any prior experience with music, they'll be starting from scratch, if they get started at all. Given the self-conscience nature of most junior high school students, music serves as a great way to draw them out. So it's immensely valuable for mentors to provide weekly music lessons to the elementary students."

These are not just wild ideas or even well summarized learning theory. The Junior University program began in 2007 and the full JULI model began in 2012, and they continue until this day. They are in our public schools, and they are working—right here in Silicon Valley, on the southern peninsula of the San Francisco Bay Area, which isn't known as the friendliest place on Earth for people of faith.

THE BIGGEST MIRACLE

No doubt many readers are wondering, *What happened to Lyn Merza?*

Following my keynote address to launch the school year on August 12, 2014, our board members, their spouses, and several friends of Valley Christian met in our chapel to hear about plans for the coming year. Jerry and Lyn were there, and I felt prompted to pray for Lyn. She gladly accepted the offer and told us she had something to say. With grateful tears she explained, "We appreciate your prayers so much because we know God hears every prayer. Earlier this year I had a recurrence of cancer. I did three rounds of chemo, and by God's grace, all tests showed I was going into remission again. Last March I had my final chemo session."

Lyn took a deep breath as she continued. "This past week I learned that the CA-125 tumor marker is up to thirty-five, the highest point of the normal range. It could be that the cancer is coming back. But now I know the Lord, and I believe He will take care of my family and me. The biggest miracle is that although cancer may not leave my body, God healed my faith. It could be that my time on earth will be shorter than I hoped, but I know I will be with Jesus forever, and I have peace because of Him. Before we came to Christ Jesus," she said with tears welling up in her eyes, "I was afraid to die. I was afraid to leave my children and Jerry behind. But I'm not afraid anymore, and it all started when the students at Valley prayed over me. And for that, I will always be grateful."

Lyn's words touched me deeply, and I knew others felt the same. I was impressed with her faith and courage, as well as her clear understanding of the immeasurable and eternal value of faith in Jesus. Lyn's newfound faith and joy in the face of her deadly cancer was truly "the biggest miracle."

Lyn continued her valiant struggle. Just over two years later, in October 2016, I had the privilege of talking and praying with Lyn in her hospital room. At one point I asked if she ever heard Jesus speaking to her during her quiet times. Her answer was amazing.

"Jesus spoke to me as I read Philippians 1:20–21 [NIV]. The verses say, 'I eagerly expect and hope that I will in no way be ashamed, but will have sufficient courage so that now as always Christ will be exalted in my body, whether by life or by death. For to me, to live is Christ and to die is gain.'" Then Lyn said, "God spoke those comforting words to me so I would know all is well, whether I live or die. I asked Him if this is it and my time to die. He told me I still have a short time to live, and then I'm going to be with Him forever." Within just a few weeks, Lyn went home to be with Jesus. She passed away on Monday, November 14, 2016, with her family at her side.

We all miss Lyn, and we can't imagine what a difficult adjustment it's been for Jerry and the children. But we remain thankful for Lyn's great faith and the comfort she had knowing she will be reunited with her family and friends in heaven. When Jerry asked me to officiate at Lyn's "celebration of life" at the VCS Skyway campus on Sunday, November 27, I felt honored. To prepare for that day, I met with Jerry, his eighth-grade daughter, Cameron, and his fifth-grade son, Brayden, in our chapel to plan the service.

Cameron said she wanted to speak about her mother's passing at the service. When I asked what we should list in the program as her topic, Cameron answered, "The Blessings of Cancer." My eyes widened, and I looked over at Jerry. He asked his daughter, "What do you want to say about the blessings of cancer, Cameron?" She replied, "I want everyone to know that without cancer, Mom might not have received Jesus as her Savior so she could be ready for all of us to be together in heaven. That's the blessings of cancer for our family. We are all Christians now because cancer brought us to believe in Jesus."

Cameron's faith greatly impressed me. Her faith and words were so much like her mother's. They reminded me of what Jesus said about the Roman centurion who asked for healing for his servant: "I have not found such great faith even in Israel."[29]

TAKING ON A NEW CHALLENGE

When his children returned to school and when Jerry was ready to get back to work, he talked with me about his professional career. "As you know, when I left Hellyer Elementary School as principal, I accepted a position as director of human resources at the Franklin-McKinley School District. But it wasn't long before I missed the atmosphere and the excitement of everything that was happening back at Hellyer. The new job has been great, but it pulled me away from working on the ground floor of the JULI programs and seeing them grow and improve." Although he loved the school district job, he said, he missed the daily interaction he'd had with the children and their dedicated teachers.

When the position of superintendent of education opened at Valley Christian Schools, the VCS board and I asked Jerry if he would consider coming to Valley and filling that role. It was a responsibility I'd held for many years, but the schools had grown dramatically, and we needed help. By this time, I had more than enough to do serving as president of VCS, the Quest Institute, and the Agape Preschools, along with a long list of other commitments. We were delighted when Jerry agreed to join the Valley team in July 2017. I was confident he would be the perfect person for the job.

Some time later, Jerry told a campus visitor, "One reason I was glad when Cliff offered me the opportunity to serve as superintendent at Valley was that I would get to be part of the JULI programs again. In this role, I'm able to connect with the Franklin–McKinley School District on a different level. I can talk with my former colleagues and assure them of our support. I've told them to let us know whatever they need, and if we can make it happen, we will. If it's not possible for us, then we'll try to find a partner school, like Andrew Hill, or other mentors who can fulfill their needs."

Read on for more inspiration about how JULI can help spread transformation to your community and public schools.

CHAPTER 6

JULI:

Junior University and the Lighthouse Initiative

VALLEY CHRISTIAN HIGH SCHOOL hosted our very first year-end Junior University awards program on the Skyway campus at the end of the 2007–2008 school year. We wanted to honor the academic achievements of Hellyer Elementary School students, so we invited San Jose Mayor Chuck Reed and Dr. John Porter, superintendent of the Franklin–McKinley School District, to help present the awards.

Dr. Porter told me, "I wish all of our graduates could have an opportunity to participate in a program like this." I was glad to hear that, but then he said something that hit home. "I wish every one of our eighth-grade graduates could have the same opportunities as students at Valley Christian High School. Our Franklin–McKinley students are so precious."

My mind raced as I thought about all the obstacles to admitting so many public school students to Valley's ninth-grade class.

"We have only about 120 open spaces in ninth grade after admitting more than three hundred of our own eighth-grade graduates," I said.

Dr. Porter's next statement surprised me. "I'm going to try and find some money to fund scholarships for some of our eighth-grade graduates to attend Valley Christian High School. These opportunities would change their lives."

I never imagined I would hear those words from a public school superintendent. I thanked him and said, "I wish we could make room and admit all of your junior high graduates. Even though it's impossible for us to take them all, what we can do is take Valley Christian into your Franklin–McKinley School District schools."

Looking back on that conversation, I don't think either of us could even begin to imagine all of the wonderful outcomes that would occur in the following years as we took that journey together. Neither of us knew at the time how to import the wonderful opportunities for students at Valley Christian Schools into our local public schools, but we wanted to make it happen.

As it turned out, the positive impact was a two-way street. We bused our students to serve as mentors at the Franklin–McKinley schools, but more always came back on the bus for our students than ever went over on the bus. That was the year we started seeing a major improvement in the achievement scores of students at Hellyer Elementary. The secret was not only that we had teenagers volunteering to tutor students in the elementary school, but it was also that someone showed an interest in each of them and established an emotional bond with them. Our teenagers were there to encourage the kids by becoming their cheerleaders, and that made all the difference.

I especially like what Dr. Porter said when he came to my office for a visit a few days later. "The children in our schools have the same capacity in their brains as those in your schools," he asserted. "It's just that they don't have the same opportunities to succeed." He was right about that. But if we sit around waiting until we can find a tax-based solution to all the problems in the public schools, we will fail. The real solution lies in the community.

By that time, the improved academic achievement of the Hellyer students was documented by standardized achievement tests. Dr. Porter saw that, and he told me, "Cliff, you need to figure out 'what's the magic?' and document it." And that's what we are doing. In fact, that's one of the important purposes of this book.

While Dr. Porter's enthusiasm was encouraging, it became very important for us to make certain we walked wisely between the First Amendment's establishment and free exercise clauses, as described earlier.

Upon reflection, I am thankful for the Supreme Court rulings— at least, I'm thankful for what they mean, properly understood. Parents don't want their children taught a politically correct religion or generic prayers "appropriate" for all religions. And regardless of their religious beliefs, parents should never support any form of coerced religious instruction by anyone, including public school educators.

The question for us is this: Will Christians and others of good will in the community take advantage of the free exercise clause to help restore the moral compass in America's classrooms? The Supreme Court made sure the government could not establish any form of religious instruction in the public schools, but our right to the free exercise of our faith remains intact, so long as people exercise their religious liberties in an appropriate and non-coercive manner.

In one of its most seminal rulings, the Supreme Court declared that students do not "shed their constitutional rights . . . at the schoolhouse gate."[30] It's crucial for our public school teachers to understand that they may not teach students to *believe* the "self-evident" truths "that all men are created equal [and] are endowed by their Creator with certain unalienable rights." However, students have the right to learn the history of how these "self-evident" truths are embedded in our founding documents.

THE EKKLESIA IN EDUCATION™

One of our newer initiatives is a religious organization founded in 2017 to challenge Christians to become more involved with our local schools. The Ekklesia in Education was established as an association of churches and other Christian organizations to help enable them to reach the children in our schools. Whether you are part of a church, a Christian school, a Christian college, a Sunday school class, or a home prayer or Bible study group, the Ekklesia in Education is a resource for Christians to rediscover and affirm the importance of letting their light shine for the children of our communities.

Moreover, the Ekklesia in Education programs are designed not only for those who self-identify as Christians but also for those we call people of good will. For example, employees at Cisco, Google, Microsoft, and other corporations help inspire and train students from economically challenged families in our local community. People of good will make amazing contributions to quality education and offer important mentoring resources.

For Christians in particular, it ought to be our prayer that every child in America would hear the truth and have a choice to follow the teachings of Jesus. And think of this: Jesus made it clear that His followers bear the responsibility to shine His light. If our public school children never learn the teachings of Jesus, the blame falls on us. Let's not be deceived into thinking that children in public schools are out of the reach of Jesus and His followers.

I often think of the multitudes who came to hear Jesus. They listened attentively to His teaching, but after a while they became hungry. Jesus' disciples thought there was nothing they could do about it. They said, "This is a remote place, and it's already getting late. Send the crowds away so they can go to the villages and buy food for themselves."

But Jesus challenged their assumptions. "That is not necessary—you feed them."[31]

Flummoxed, one of them replied, "There is a lad here who has five barley loaves and two small fish, but what are they among so many?"[32] If Jesus had had the same mindset as His disciples, the story would have ended there. Instead, He told them to bring Him what they had.

After He looked to heaven and blessed the small offering, He broke the loaves "into pieces" and then "gave the bread to the disciples, who distributed it to the people." The text says Jesus and His disciples fed about five thousand men that day, "in addition to all the women and children!"[33]

The disciples quickly understood that Jesus had commanded them to feed the great crowd with only one boy's lunch of five loaves and two fish. What the disciples learned—on two different occasions[34]—was that Jesus has the resources to feed the multitudes through them. They just needed to believe and obey His commands.

Some people have the mindset that quality education for all children in the nation is impossible. But when we embrace the idea that Jesus will do His miraculous works by His power through us for all of our children, then, just as He fed the multitudes, He will enable us to offer quality education to all children in our schools.

At VCS, we often call on the work Dr. Ed Silvoso has pioneered, including the central message of his book *Prayer Evangelism*, which focuses on how to reclaim business, government, and education with the transformative teachings of Christ. As Christian educators, we believe our calling is to serve all children in our communities, not just those who come to our churches or attend our Christian schools. We've applied Jesus' prayer evangelism concepts, and they became the foundation for Junior University and the Lighthouse Initiative to reclaim the next generation.

I hope every reader of this book will come to see how true the words of Jesus are regarding our responsibility to the children in our schools. He told His disciples, "You are the light of the world."[35] We are the light bearers. If the children in our schools are struggling in darkness, it's because Christians have failed to shine the light. Changing this situation will require an intensive infusion of Christian service and prayer. Praying individuals and intercessory groups for the children in every school will push back the darkness to allow every child to hear the truth and have a choice to follow Jesus.

DISCOVERING THE STRONG FOUNDATION

The Common Virtues offer a bright light to warm the fertile soil of every student's soul. These ideas about nurturing the soul are not new. Nearly twenty-five hundred years ago, Socrates declared, "All men's souls are immortal, but the souls of the righteous are immortal and divine."[36] Wise and great teachers have always insisted that true success and well-being rely not only on the acquisition of knowledge but also on the acquisition and application of virtue and strong moral character. Plato said, "Education is teaching our children to desire the right things."[37] And America's first president, George Washington, declared, "Human happiness and moral duty are inseparably connected."[38]

Regarding the birth of our nation, President Washington penned these words in a letter:

> I receive with the greater satisfaction your congratulations on the establishment of the new constitution of government, because I believe its mild yet efficient operations will . . . confirm the hopes of its numerous friends; and because the moderation, patriotism, and wisdom of the present federal Legislature seem to promise the restoration of order and our ancient virtues, the extension of genuine religion, and the consequent advancement of our respectability abroad, and of our substantial happiness at home.[39]

Washington could thankfully place his confidence in the qualities of the legislature to restore "order and our ancient virtues, the extension of genuine religion," because all three branches of government remain deeply rooted in the checks and balances provided by our nation's Constitution.

But how can a practical application of a Common Virtues Initiative work in our public schools? Junior University and the Lighthouse Initiative (JULI), developed at Valley Christian Schools for interaction with the local public schools, offer a proven model for Christians everywhere to follow.

JULI, as we have discussed, represents two distinct programs that work together to achieve the best results. The first, Junior University, operates during the school day with a secular vocabulary in compliance with the establishment clause of the First Amendment. The second, the Lighthouse Initiative, operates after school with parent permission, in compliance with the First Amendment's free exercise clause. These programs combine into one initiative like the two doorposts of a schoolhouse door. I describe it as the door of opportunity for our children. When it's working well, the door opens for positive student opportunities and closes to negative student influences. But the JULI door doesn't work as well unless both doorposts (Junior University and the Lighthouse Initiative) are in place and the door remains firmly attached to its hinges, which represent the legacy of Common Virtues of our nation's Founding Fathers, as described in the Declaration of Independence.

The following table shows how the language used in these programs has applications in both secular and faith-based environments, and how these two programs work side by side. They become most effective for promoting a positive school culture of Light, Life, and Learning when combined into one initiative. Keep in mind that both Junior University and the Lighthouse Initiative are programs offered by volunteer mentors. Both programs can offer the same enriched academic, artistic, and athletic instruction, such as choir, dance, instrumental music lessons, robotics, International Space Station experiments, and team sports. The Lighthouse Initiative can also offer a weekly Kids Club Bible program and can integrate Christian truths into all of the enrichment activities with parent permission. During the school day, Junior University mentors use secular vocabulary as reflected in the ten principles on the lower left side of the table, and after-school Lighthouse mentors may use a Christian faith vocabulary as shown in the ten statements on the right side of the table.

JUNIOR UNIVERSITY	LIGHTHOUSE
Celebrating a Culture of Goodness, Peace, and Joy	Celebrating a Culture of Goodness, Peace, and Joy
All Students – During School	Parent Permission – After School
Public School – Secular Vocabulary	Public School – Faith Vocabulary
Light, Life, and Learning – Curriculum Adoption*	Christian Virtues & *Light, Life, and Learning*
Founding Fathers' Values and Common Virtues in the Declaration of Independence	Bible Lessons, Prayer, Common Virtues in the Declaration of Independence

A3

ACADEMIC ACHIEVEMENT ·	ARTISTIC BEAUTY ·	ATHLETIC DISTINCTION
A. Classroom Hydroponics	A. Art	1. Learn to Swim Lessons
B. ISS Experiments	B. Band – Instr. Lessons	2. Nutrition
C. Reading Buddies & Tutoring	C. Cheer, Dance – Flags	3. Skill Development
D. Robotics	D. Choir	4. Team Sports

Light, Life, and Learning Curriculum – TheQuestInstitute.com

JUNIOR UNIVERSITY	LIGHTHOUSE
1. Teachers and JULI volunteers model respect for younger students in view of every person's priceless, incredible, and equal value	1. High school student volunteers teach Bible stories, to emphasize God's love for all and that all people have infinite value
2. Students learn to respect themselves and others because all are equally priceless	2. Students learn to love God and their neighbors as themselves
3. Students learn that academic achievement empowers them to transform their community and the world through goodness, peace, and joy	3. Students learn through prayer and academic achievement to transform their community and the world through God's love
4. Every student has unique gifts that emerge as gifted passions when discovered and developed	4. Every student has God-given gifts that emerge as gifted passions when discovered and developed
5. As mentors, high school students help offer comprehensive learning opportunities to enable elementary students to discover and develop their gifts and emerging passions	5. As mentors, high school students help offer comprehensive learning opportunities to enable elementary students to discover and develop their God-given gifts and emerging passions
6. Mentors model goodness, peace, and joy to feed the hearts of young elementary student mentees to inspire accelerated student learning	6. Mentors model faith, hope, and love, feeding the soul with goodness, peace, and joy to inspire and enrich the minds and hearts of students to learn
7. Teachers challenge students to fly with their dreams to pass on goodness, peace, and joy to others and to transform the world into a better place by helping others	7. Mentors challenge students to share God's goodness, peace, and joy with others to positively transform the world because Jesus loves everyone
8. Parents are valued as the primary educators of their children	8. Parents are valued as the primary educators of their children under God
9. Good character is an expression of Common Virtues to others	9. Christian character is an expression of God's goodness to others
10. The community celebrates the achievements of all students as they prepare themselves to serve as transformers with good character to transform their communities and the world	10. The community celebrates the achievements of all students as they prepare themselves to serve as transformers with Christian character to transform their communities and the world

When VCS began partnering with Hellyer Elementary School, we realized that without developing strong moral character, "human happiness" will be lacking for our children, just as George Washington warned. In our Christian schools, the energy for a positive school culture—one of mutual respect, a passion for learning, and innovation—rests on a solid foundation of Christian faith. But as we discovered, the legacy of the Declaration of Independence offers Common Virtues and a moral compass for our public schools. As we introduced these truths to students, we were pleasantly surprised by their powerful impact on student achievement and the school culture.

More than three centuries after those first American settlers arrived on our shores, Ronald Reagan, then California's governor and later U.S. president, recalled the words of Pilgrim leader John Winthrop while giving an address in the nation's capital:

> Standing on the tiny deck of the Arabella in 1630 off the Massachusetts coast, John Winthrop said, "We will be as a city upon a hill. The eyes of all people are upon us, so that if we deal falsely with our God in this work we have undertaken and so cause Him to withdraw His present help from us, we shall be made a story and a byword throughout the world."

Then Reagan said, "Well, we have not dealt falsely with our God, even if He is temporarily suspended from the classroom." And he added, ". . . we are today, the last best hope of man on earth."[40]

President Reagan's words ought to remind us of where this nation began and where we stand today. The vision of that "shining city on a hill" is still strong, even as we work overtime to restore the Common Virtues in our schools. The challenge has never been greater, and we must not deny the importance of our efforts to offer quality education to the next generation.

HOW TRANSFORMATION HAPPENS

When Principal Jerry Merza saw the impact of the programs he and Cindy Nardi developed at Hellyer Elementary, he said he could hardly believe his eyes. As the student volunteers from Valley Christian High School began sharing a Christian message through the after-school enrichment programs and Kids Club, the culture of the school began to change in remarkable ways.

"Before we developed the JULI programs," Jerry said, "some of our upper-grade students pushed the envelope with their bad behavior. But JULI changed all of that. We had an artist paint a beautiful sixty-foot mural on one of the large blank walls in front of the school with every word of the preamble to the Declaration of Independence. It was right at the front gate, and it helped bring new pride to the school.

"Our students loved learning about the Declaration. They even talked about it when they were outside, not just in class, saying that they're all created equal and endowed by their Creator with certain unalienable rights. What I saw on the playground and in the cafeteria was a transformation of the students' attitudes. And one of the most gratifying parts was how the older students began seeing themselves as role models to the younger children."

Hellyer Elementary helped beta-test a key resource Cindy Nardi and I co-authored: a curriculum for elementary school students called *Light, Life, and Learning*. It's a booklet educators and volunteers anywhere can use with children in our schools, and it includes hands-on projects the students can develop. In writing the curriculum, we wanted children to know there are goals they can attain. We wanted to bring faith and hope to places often filled with hopelessness and disappointment.

Light, Life, and Learning features four to five approximately forty-five-minute lessons, depending on the age group, with inspiring stories about people who represent the values of the Light, Life, and Learning paradigm, to encourage and inform elementary students. Colorful characters and drawings illustrate the curriculum. The twenty-page storybook reveals Common Virtues through the life examples of Paul Revere, Mother Theresa, Dr. Martin Luther King Jr., Cesar Chavez, and the great English statesman William Wilberforce. It's a fun program for young students. Projection slides are available with the book.

The curriculum is personal and practical. An accompanying kit includes exercises, projects, and puzzles the children can work on to illustrate the critical concepts in the book and contains all the pieces for the object lessons. As the children read these stories and do the exercises, they come to understand their innate value as well as the legacy of faith and freedom handed down through the Declaration of Independence.

The goal is to engage the children at an earlier age with the Junior University character development emphasis. When students come to understand how special they are, you can see it in their eyes. They come alive, and their emotional reservoirs seem to overflow. Then they're ready to learn. The picture book is colorful and engaging for students, and easy and fun for teachers to teach. The messages get applied in clear and easily accessible ways. Going through each of the lessons with a set of activities and assessments provides a rich learning opportunity for students because they enjoy the stories and the projects.

The activities include object lessons like the uniqueness of every snowflake to illustrate how unique and precious every child is, and how this truth applies to every person. Students take part in an exercise to create their unique paper snowflakes, and they soon discover what uniqueness means and how no two snowflakes are alike. These and other elements of the curriculum help teach the principles of good character and Common Virtues. And, best of all, the lessons help the children understand their unique value and why it's important to treat everyone with kindness because everyone is of equal value. The *Light, Life, and Learning* curriculum is available at TheQuestInstitute.com.

WHY CHARACTER COUNTS

The passage from the California Education Code I referred to in Chapter Two, from Section 233.5(a), requires all educators in the state to impress upon students the principles of character and morality. Clauses (a) and (b) read:

(a) Each teacher shall endeavor to impress upon the minds of the pupils the principles of morality, truth, justice, patriotism, and a true comprehension of the rights, duties, and dignity of American citizenship, and the meaning of equality and human dignity, including the promotion of harmonious relations, kindness toward domestic pets and the humane treatment of living creatures, to teach them to avoid idleness, profanity, and falsehood, and to instruct them in manners and morals and the principles of a free government.

(b) Each teacher is also encouraged to create and foster an environment that encourages pupils to realize their full potential and that is free from discriminatory attitudes, practices, events, or activities, in order to prevent acts of hate violence. . . .[41]

The California Department of Education requires character education especially for elementary schools, saying:

Effective schools seek to develop and reinforce character traits, such as caring, citizenship, fairness, respect, responsibility, and trustworthiness, through a systematic approach that includes adult modeling, curriculum integration, a positive school climate, and access to comprehensive guidance and counseling services.[42]

At least thirty-six states have legislated the inclusion of character education requirements in their public schools, and seven others support character education in various ways without a legal mandate. According to a report by Character.org, only seven states, including Idaho, Massachusetts, Nevada, New Hampshire, New Mexico, Wisconsin, and Wyoming, have no legislation specifically addressing the need for schools to offer character education to all children.[43]

Lessons about the importance of character development come from many sources, and I ran across a wonderful quote from U.S. President Theodore Roosevelt, who held office from 1901 to 1909, that makes the case very well. Teddy Roosevelt was known as a rugged outdoorsman, and he once declared in a popular magazine of the day, "Bodily vigor is good, and vigor of intellect is even better, but far above both is character." He then added, ". . . no brilliancy of intellect, no perfection of bodily development, will count when weighed in the balance against that assemblage of virtues, active and passive, of moral qualities, which we group together under the name of character."[44]

When our local public school principals and I began meeting weekly in 2012, we agreed that teaching character is important in our schools. They explained how difficult it was for their schools to adopt a character development curriculum. They asked for any ideas we could offer, given the mandate to avoid teaching Christian faith or any religious bias. In our pluralistic society, we have many and varied belief systems and many religious communities. The desire to extend respect to all and not offend anyone made the adoption of a single character development program particularity challenging.

What we have discovered since, however, is the *Light, Life, and Learning* curriculum, which gives teachers and resource specialists an actionable character education program that meets the requirements in California and other states. The curriculum affirms the legacy of the Declaration of Independence. It is ideal for teaching patriotism, the basis for human rights, and good citizenship, including equality, human dignity, harmonious relations, manners, morals, and respect. It encourages a positive school culture of kindness and exemplary behavior. Each lesson brings Common Virtues into focus and helps develop good character.

GETTING STARTED: THE SEVEN-STEP JULI MODEL

To help you get started, we'd like to share Seven Proven Steps for implementing Junior University and the Lighthouse Initiative in your neighborhood schools. Having read this far in the book, many may be excited to implement the JULI model. We offer a few words of caution spoken so eloquently by Principal Jerry Merza: "Just don't go into the school with an agenda. The last message principals and teachers want to hear from anyone is what a lousy job they're doing and how you've come to fix their problems. You're not going to make it past the receptionist with that kind of approach."

1. PRAY for the students and educators in your neighborhood school. Ask God to call and appoint prayer intercessors to meet regularly to pray for the students, educators, and families in your neighborhood school(s).

2. SHARE the VISION: It is God's vision that empowers His plans. Proceed with confidence and speak with boldness.

3. MEET the PRINCIPAL: Commend the school principal and teachers for their committed efforts to nurture and educate their students with limited resources.

4. MAKE a PLAN with the PRINCIPAL: The principal is likely to begin slowly to build trust. Opportunities to work directly with students may come later. Select and agree on your project and what you will accomplish.

5. RECRUIT TRUSTED VOLUNTEERS to implement the plan. After winning confidence and trust, don't hesitate to look for opportunities to integrate Christian faith in programs offered before or after school with signed permission from parents.

6. CELEBRATE with PARENTS: All parents love to see their children succeed, achieve their dreams, and walk with confidence into their destiny.

7. ASSESS, DOCUMENT, REFINE, and REPEAT: At the conclusion of every project, meet with your school leadership. Assess and document your methods and accomplishments with possible improvements for the next opportunity to serve.

Here are some examples of mentoring ideas that are working well in our Silicon Valley schools. Your school principal may request similar programs:

✧ A monthly lunch provided for teachers and staff

✧ The *Light, Life, and Learning* character development curriculum, including four to five approximate forty-five-minute lessons (available at TheQuestInstitute.com)

✧ A tutoring program, or the Reading Buddies program (mentors read with mentees, often English-language learners)

✧ The International Space Station program for students in fourth grade and higher. Grants may be available for schools with disadvantaged socioeconomic circumstances. See vimeo.com/142988653 and TheQuest Institute.com/programs/quest-for-space, or search for "Quest for Space" or "The Quest Institute"

✧ Sponsoring classroom hydroponic gardening projects (more about hydroponics in the next chapter)

✧ Weekly instrumental music lessons from community volunteers during and after school hours (consider a jazz band as students develop their skills)

✧ A children's choir that features "The Declaration Song." Children may listen to the song playing during class while they are doing their classwork. The Quest Institute for Quality Education offers "The Declaration Song" without cost. See vimeo.com/261758685

"At Hellyer Elementary," Jerry said, "the kids learn 'The Declaration Song,' starting in first grade. It's a song using the exact words of the preamble to the Declaration of Independence, and they love it. I hear them singing the song all over campus, even when they're alone, just walking around by themselves. Many times the parents don't know their kids have learned it, so when we do a concert program where the moms and dads can hear their children singing that song, some parents burst into tears because they are so proud. I have tears in my eyes just thinking about it. The kids sing it with such enthusiasm. They're so proud of their accomplishments."

✧ Lighthouse after-school enrichment programs with parent permission, including possible robotics, art, photography, cheer, dance, swim, or other athletic programs (see the table on page 117) and a Kids Club Bible program (see KidsClubConsultants.org)

✧ A large mural at the school entry or other prominent location, funded and commissioned by volunteers, that features the preamble to the Declaration of Independence with all of the wording exactly as written in the Declaration

✧ An end-of-the-year event for the children and their parents to display the accomplishments of students (for example, demonstrating their new dance, band, art, or robotic skills), including an annual performance of the Declaration song with added patriotic songs

While offering these programs during the school day, be certain to integrate Common Virtues based on the "self-evident" truths that all "are created equal" and "are endowed by their Creator with certain unalienable rights," including "life, liberty, and the pursuit of happiness." These truths can serve as an affirmative message and a strong moral authority to shape a positive school culture of goodness, peace, and joy. They also offer a solid guidance system to explain to students why each of them should view himself or herself as having tremendous value, with a purpose for living and equal respect for others. For after-school programs, Christians may legally integrate Christian faith truths and prayer into any of these programs, with parent permission.

It's important to celebrate student success at the end of a semester or school year. We invite parents, relatives, and their friends for students to showcase their achievements at a concert, followed by a carnival, with food for all. Parents love to see their children succeed, achieve their dreams, and walk with confidence into their future. Students perform in the jazz band, sing in the choir, dance, show their artwork and robots, perform cheerleading routines, display ISS experiments, and receive enthusiastic and well-deserved applause. The event gives them recognition for the interest, determination, and effort they've put into learning new skills. When everybody cheers, and when their parents are out there in the audience taking smartphone photos and videos, the children can bask in much needed praise, admiration, and appreciation.

CHAPTER 7

TURNING ON THE LIGHT:
REALIZING YOU CAN
MAKE A DIFFERENCE

"FROM DEEP SPACE to the ocean depths."

This phrase is more than a motto for the Quest Institute for Quality Education. School programs such as the Quest for Space experiments on the International Space Station (ISS), the Quest for Oceans deep-sea experiments, and the Ocean Discovery competition, which I will describe in more detail shortly, are opening up previously unknown opportunities for the young people taking part in these initiatives. And other programs such as hydroponic farming offer an even broader range of learning options.

Think of it as a triangle: First, Valley Christian Schools incubates and delivers Applied Math, Science, and Engineering (AMSE) projects and other opportunities for VCS students. Then the Quest Institute for Quality Education helps scale Valley's prototype programs as a conduit for schools around the world. Lastly, the Ekklesia in Education challenges Christian professionals and people of good will who want to help provide opportunities to students by serving as mentors, coaches, and tutors. The Ekklesia mandate is to get them involved and connected with students.

As we were formulating these ideas, someone said, "Okay, you guys are doing something great. But how are you going to make other people interested to the point they'll actually do it?" We think these three pathways are a big part of the answer. If we can help people see the results they can achieve when they connect with students, I believe they'll want to get involved. And when they realize they are needed, they should have even more incentive when they learn they don't have to quit their jobs or get a teaching credential to inspire young people to greatness.

For Christians there's an even broader perspective because, as stated in the last chapter, we also have a divine responsibility to influence the world with God's goodness, peace, and joy, as Jesus commanded.[45] But the achievers in almost all professions have knowledge that can help transform the lives of the young people in our schools, and sharing with the coming generation of leaders is a privilege true professionals don't want to miss.

The Quest Institute opportunities are great pathways involving science, technology, engineering, and math, so a certain level of experience in those fields is helpful for those willing to serve as mentors. But the Quest Institute offers training for achievers who don't have an extensive STEM background, showing them how to mentor students in the Quest programs.

There are multiple pathways for involvement for mentors who are not experts in math or science—almost as many kinds of opportunities as there are schools. Every potential mentor will have at least one pathway where that person can make a difference in the future success of children who lack opportunities.

For instance, some local senior citizens learned that students at Andrew Hill High School wanted to go to the student-led Christian Club during lunch hour but faced a roadblock. Christian students are able to share their faith with other students in the club, but most students didn't have food to bring from home for lunch. They relied on the federally funded free school lunch program, and by the time they stood in line to get their meal, little time remained to eat and get to their next class. So they had a choice: Either skip lunch, or miss the Christian Club meetings. As a result, usually only a few students would attend the Christian Club.

But, thankfully, these senior citizens went to the school, met the officers of the Christian Club, and discovered the problem. They began bringing food for the weekly meetings, and attendance suddenly increased, with as many as eighty students attending each week. During one meeting, more than thirty high school students prayed to receive Jesus as their Lord and Savior when they were given the opportunity by another student.

There are so many reasons why it's important for mentors to engage with the schools. Evidence backs a growing consensus that our schools need to produce more engineers, not only to raise the standard of living for their families, but also to reduce our nation's reliance on international engineers. Rob Valiton, the COO of VCS and a Silicon Valley executive and engineer, described how thousands of engineering graduates from other countries come to the United States each year to work. They learn our language and technology, but quite a few of them decide to return home, and they take the knowledge they've gained with them.

The reality is that America's schools are not producing enough engineers from our own student population to satisfy the need. Adults who have had success in their careers ought to be mentoring these students, helping to turn on the light to their potential. The young people need encouragement and hope. Again, it's the same Light, Life, and Learning paradigm.

Some would respond, "Well, that's the teacher's responsibility." And, in part, that's true. Teachers are trained as subject matter experts to teach U.S. history, algebra, calculus, English literature, and other disciplines. But think of this: You will rarely find even one engineer, entrepreneur, concert pianist, corporate innovator, scientist, or successful business leader teaching in our schools. The men and women who have taken the time to obtain their teaching credentials are accomplished teachers, but few are accomplished entrepreneurs, corporate leaders, or scientific innovators. Moreover, parents who have not been in a position to achieve such professional ambitions often have no way of knowing how to help their children. That's why it is so important to connect the millions of schoolchildren who don't have opportunities to discover their innate skills and abilities with the professionals in their communities who can show them the way.

The Quest Institute for Quality Education has a pathway, and at this moment that pathway includes three separate research opportunities: the ISS program, the underwater research program in cooperation with the Monterey Bay Aquarium Research Institute, and the new hydroponic experiments with plants. And more programs are in the works, including a Quest for Health and Wellness Initiative in cooperation with Dr. Eric Phelps, who serves Valley Christian as president of the board of directors. Dr. Phelps and his colleagues are planning to involve VCS students in developing and administering a screening protocol to identify elementary children with breathing disorders. We are constantly exploring and incubating new STEM projects for our students at Valley Christian Schools, with an aim to make them available to students everywhere through the Quest Institute for Quality Education.

FULL FAITH AND CONFIDENCE

At this point many readers might be thinking, *WOW! I'd really like to help make some of these Quest Institute opportunities available to the students in our local school, but I could never mentor students like Silicon Valley engineers.*

Well, I have some great news for you. This part of the book will tell you why you can proceed with full faith and confidence that volunteer mentors and their student mentees will be successful in your community. In addition to both volunteer and contracted talent, a growing team of full-time engineers and technologists support Quest Institute initiatives being implemented around the world. As of this writing, the team includes these professionals:

✧ **Stephen Huber** is an accomplished engineer who leads our Quest for Space ISS program and Quest for Oceans program as an associate director of research and development.

✧ **Howell Ivy** was a division president and deputy COO of Sega Enterprises, USA, overseeing all hardware development. Howell engineered the Level III advanced CubeLab solution. Howell also serves on the Quest for Space team that developed our NexGen ISS program.

✧ **Danny Kim** serves as the chief technology officer of the Quest Institute and Director of AMSE. His responsibility is to oversee a team of engineers to develop extraordinary math, science, and engineering career pathways for Valley Christian students and for member schools of the Quest Institute. Danny is co-founder and CTO of FullArmor Corporation, the security software firm he and his partners founded in 1990. Danny's personal experiences with each of these programs, and his amazing partnership with Microsoft, a FullArmor client, make for fascinating reading, as you will see for yourself in the next chapter.

✧ **Hannah Kim** earned her M.A. at the Harvard University Graduate School of Education. She is the founding VP/Director of Valley Christian Schools Business and Entrepreneurship Initiative where she developed and leads the President's Business Challenge. Hannah also serves as the Director of Education for the Quest for Space program, and oversees the Quest for Space curriculum development and product distribution.

✧ **Dan Saldana** had a career at Lockheed, working with NASA. He headed eighty-nine satellite projects, mostly secret projects for the U.S. Department of Defense. Dan now serves as International Space Station (ISS) project leader at Valley Christian High School, where he has assisted students in placing 160 (and counting) experiments on the ISS.

✧ **George Sousa** is a physicist whose engineering career included building nuclear power plants around the world for General Electric. He helped develop the VCS rocketry program and has mentored students as they design and build multi-stage seventeen-foot rockets. George enthusiastically supports and mentors students in a variety of Quest Institute programs.

✧ **Rob Valiton** is an engineer and former senior vice president at Atmel Corporation. For many years Rob traveled the world for this telecom giant, which is now part of Verizon. Rob is COO of the Quest for Space program.

Not one of these amazing and accomplished people employed at Valley Christian is here because they need a job. They don't. They are here to use their knowledge and influence to help shape the next generation. I've often heard comments such as, "I'm nowhere near retirement age, but I want to do something meaningful with my life by investing in the next generation." That's their legacy.

Not every community can supply volunteers like these, but this level of talent and capability can be accessed in every community because these experts have helped the Quest Institute create and package programs that can be adopted and used by schools anywhere.

All the components in our programs are tested and proved in real-time educational applications in our local schools and organizations before they're offered to others. Our commitment is to make them available and accessible to young people everywhere at reasonable costs with lots of technical support. You don't have to be a Stanford engineer to provide the ISS program to students in your community. You can do it with the training and materials created and delivered by the Quest Institute, because the systems are perfected by engineers to work in fourth grade through university.

When Lan Nguyen, a fourth- and fifth-grade teacher at Hellyer Elementary school, heard about the Quest for Space and the opportunity for her students to build and place experiments on the International Space Station, she was excited and apprehensive at the same time. She was excited by how the ISS program could transform the way young people think about education, science, themselves, and their future aspirations and careers. And she was terrified about trying to lead her students to literally build and send their experiments into space. In the face of her fears, she courageously signed up for the program.

After her training she exclaimed, "My major is in social welfare and education. I'm not a technical person at all. I don't know anything about circuits or electricity, but in three days I have done it all. I was coding, and I've never coded in my life."

Lan was the first public elementary school teacher to sign up for the program. She integrated the hands-on ISS Quest for Space curriculum into her science curriculum to help meet California's Next Generation Science Standards (NGSS). Her students and parents were so thrilled that she agreed to teach fifth-grade students the following year and to help extend the program to more teachers and students.

When I had an opportunity to visit Lan's classroom, I was so impressed by her fourth- and fifth-grade STEM scientists working in their research teams. They were totally and enthusiastically engaged with learning. Tomorrow's scientists and engineers were passionately doing real science experiments that the students were determined to place on the ISS.

Later when I met individually with Lan, I asked about her stress level and the challenges she faced. She described how she was as enthused as the students and how successful everyone felt. She said, "The technical support from Quest is amazing. I'd advise every teacher to keep their laptop open with the Quest website's live online support. Teachers from participating schools help each other online, and we have more support from Quest engineers if needed. Every time I've had a glitch, I go to the online community and get instant answers to keep my students moving. I love it. I've never had an unresolved issue."

OVERCOMING OBJECTIONS

Danny Kim offered some very insightful comments about finding talented volunteer mentors. I want to share them before we dive into his section of the book dealing with the Quest for Space, Quest for Oceans, and other AMSE programs. Keep in mind that Danny began as a mentor with hundreds of volunteer hours before being hired to lead AMSE and the Quest Institute as CTO.

Danny explains, "Whenever we talk with young professionals, they have the same desire to make a difference as I do, but they don't know how to engage, and they don't realize what a huge difference they can make in the lives of students. They don't have a framework for connecting with students.

"I've heard them say, 'I want to give back, but I have a job. There's no time other than during the day when I'm at work that I can give to mentor.' They have a pent-up desire to contribute, but they don't have an outlet for it. Not only that, they want to learn how to make a difference. I have made it a point to reach out to them, and when these young technologists realize that the principles we're teaching students are the same ones they work and live by, they're just amazed, and they welcome the opportunity to get involved."

That's such great news, and important for many reasons. Danny leads a Bible study group at his church, and he told me he wanted to reach out to the younger people in the Bay Area who are skeptical about the Christian faith. So he decided to try something new. He set up lawn chairs outside the church because he realized some people might be interested in what they were doing there but not feel comfortable stepping inside the church building. He put up a sign announcing "Free food and discussion."

"Now, this is a Korean church," Danny told me. "We speak English, but it's mainly Korean people. But because of this new approach, a Spanish-speaking lady joined the group, then a Brazilian man became a member, and several young professionals were curious enough to take a seat and just listen. We were talking about how to apply biblical principles to your daily life and career, and I could see that some of these people were genuinely excited to learn how they could integrate faith into their daily lives.

"A few of our new enquiring friends were believers," Danny explained. "Most were seekers, but one new friend had never attended church even once in his life. Many people in the Bay Area do not attend church for personal reasons, but they're still open to ideas that may be helpful to their lives. So when I talked about things like innovation, integrity, strategic initiatives, time management, entrepreneurialism, and delegation, they were incredulous at first, and they would ask, 'Does the Bible really talk about topics like that?' So I gave them some biblical examples. I wasn't preaching at them, but I could show them specific passages in Scripture addressing those ideas. And because the correlation was so clear, even the most reluctant skeptics gained respect.

"In the beginning, the guy who had never been to church would say, 'The Bible is just a bunch of old stories with no relevance for today.' But I was able to explain it a bit more, and I would say, 'God is our Creator, and the Bible is the owner's manual He gave us to show how the people He made can be the happiest and most fulfilled during our journey on Earth.' When I shared these thoughts with them, it was really eye-opening.

"Then as we were going through all these discussions, they were especially surprised to learn that we teach the same strategies we use in our personal and professional lives to children in all of our schools. Suddenly they saw how they could get involved and give back. The QUEST for Excellence is a universal language with common principles for all successful professionals."

Danny Kim has plenty more good stories. From here until the end of this chapter, he will tell in his own words about several exciting initiatives and how they have transformed both the students and the mentors involved. And you will hear from Danny again in the next chapter.

LEARNING FROM THE BEST

One of the programs incubated at Valley Christian High School in cooperation with the Quest Institute was designed especially for business students. It's called the President's Business Challenge (PBC). Dr. Daugherty initiated the program in 2014.

The PBC, which is headed by my wife, Hannah Kim, helps students to learn and develop the skills to start a company of their own. In some ways it's like the TV program "Shark Tank." At the end of each school year, Kevin Compton, a leading Silicon Valley venture capitalist (VC), invites the finalist PBC teams to his Palo Alto offices to pitch their start-up business plans. In this case, the "millionaire judges" in addition to Mr. Compton are Steve Nelson, from the Harvard Business School, and Chi-Hua Chien, co-founder and managing partner of Goodwater Capital.

Leading up to the competition, mentors with high-level business experience teach students the basics of product ideation, development, marketing, and capital acquisition. What's more important, they also teach them the ethics and principles that go into running a successful business. They give them a holistic picture of what it means to manage a start-up organization, but with the right set of principles and guidelines in mind.

Instead of throwing college graduates out into the world of business where they learn bad habits—finding ways to get ahead with shortcuts that never last—Hannah and her associates are trying to give high school students principles that will enhance and enrich their lives. When they're at the high school level learning how to organize an ethical and efficient company, they're learning valuable life lessons, not only for their emerging careers but for their personal lives as well. When the students learn from someone like Kevin coming in and talking about his faith, and then hear that he was an early investor in Google and several other high-tech firms, suddenly they're on board. And the list goes on, with many speakers like Pat Gelsinger, CEO of VMware, and Angela Ahrendts, Senior Vice President of Retail at Apple, Inc.

Men and women at this level have a lot of knowledge and insights to share, and even the most reluctant student skeptics are impressed. They discover that you can be successful not in spite of your faith beliefs but because of them. So we say to prospective mentors, "You can share the same principles you apply in your business with your student mentees and explain to students in the schools how they can apply those principles in their daily lives. You can mentor the next generation of principled innovators."

The truth is, many people in the younger generations today are what Dr. Daugherty would call idea-deprived. They have a sense there must be something out there they're missing. They are seeking answers, and the churches haven't reached them. They're hungry for something that will give meaning to their lives.

I had an opportunity to give a talk at an event in San Francisco called a "Meetup." There are Meetups for all sorts of things: different products, different jobs, and different ideas. This one was for Christians working in the high-tech careers that are common in Silicon Valley. I was curious to see who would show up. As it turned out, more than fifty people came, from Facebook, Google, Amazon, Apple, eBay, and many of the various high-profile companies in the Bay Area. I spoke about my own journey as my partners and I started our company, FullArmor Corporation, and how we integrated our faith-based principles and values in our business and careers.

When they asked me what I'm doing, I told them I run a software company but I also work full-time for a school, because I have a passion for educating the next generation. I said that one of the programs we have enables students to come up with a science experiment and put it on board the International Space Station. When they heard that, the lights came on. In every case, the people I've told about these kinds of programs say to me, "How can I get involved?" It's something they would like to do because they know it will use their God-given talents and abilities.

That idea resonates so well with them, I believe, because these people are looking for something that will allow them to make a difference. They want their lives to matter. I ended the first session of the Meetup by saying, "Can you imagine the impact you can have when you take what you've learned and model that for a young person in the schools? That's a lifelong impact." Afterward, four or five people came up to me and asked, "Danny, how can I volunteer?"

What this tells me is that there's a pent-up desire to give back. But here's the difference: These young professionals don't want to give back in the traditional way. The church has always told them they can contribute their service, but they don't want to do food kitchens. They don't want to do manual labor. They don't want to do IT for churches. Those things don't directly impact the next generation with their gifts and talents, so they don't engage. They're like, "I'm done with that. It's antiquated."

This outlook is equally true for Christians and non-Christians alike, and here's where the "quest" part of the Quest for Quality Education comes in. It's such an attractive option for everyone involved, not just for the students but for the wider circle of professionals who can engage with the kids and serve as mentors. In so many cases, the adults are transformed too, as they come to appreciate how life-changing these programs and their influence are for their mentees, as well as for the mentees' families for generations to come.

The Quest Institute's programs, including Junior University and the Lighthouse Initiative, appeal to successful people in all types of careers and in all parts of the country. One of my lead engineers was a successful VP of a tech company in the Bay Area who quit his job because, as he said, "I believe in this." Even though he wasn't a Christian, he understood the transformative nature of what was happening with the Quest programs. That's why at VCS we talk about "Christians and people of good will." Christians have scripture-based reasons to care for the next generation, but they're not alone in their concern.

In addition to investing in the market, my associate was investing in the next generation by quitting his job. He helped revamp the ISS program to the scalable version we have today, and he's still involved. He gives us half his time and then does other projects with the rest of his time. This is what we're talking about when Cliff and I share this vision with people who want to make a difference. They want their lives to matter, and we have ways for that to happen.

Some people might say, "Okay, this is very impressive, and it works very well in Silicon Valley where you have so many top-level engineers and creative thinkers. But how is this going to work in other cities and towns that don't necessarily have the same corporate and high-tech environment?" The answer is that these are universal principles, which apply everywhere and at any time. It's important to understand that these principles have relevance not only in education but in everyone's personal life and career.

All over the world and in communities of every size, you can find examples of people following the QUEST for Excellence principles. Successful medical professionals, grocers, insurance agents, and business owners—they all have their knowledge to share. Almost all accomplished professionals follow the same principles of success, and they are candidates for having a huge impact on children in their local schools. When combined with programs like those offered through the Quest Institute, their influence can extend literally beyond Earth into space and to the ocean depths. Please take some time to review the Twenty Indispensable Principles we have discovered during our QUEST for Excellence journeys, right after the Conclusion of this book.

THE OCEAN DISCOVERY CHALLENGE

The Quest Institute for Quality Education has three main programs now to get people involved in reaching the next generation, and they're each in different stages. The Quest for Space ISS program is the most fully developed. We've proved that it works, we're scaling it out, and it is now being used in schools around the world. Schools can order a box with all the parts, and we have a curriculum that goes with it. This program is polished and very professional.

The Quest for Oceans research initiatives developed next, out of the Ocean Discovery challenge. That exciting story follows. Later I will describe our newest program, featuring hydroponics.

The Shell Ocean Discovery XPRIZE challenge began because of our success with the ISS program. Microsoft was one of our early partners, and when they saw how well the ISS program was going, they came to us and said, "You guys ought to take a look at this undersea mapping challenge. It's so hard we don't think many people will try for the prize. But since your team can develop a successful program of experiments on the International Space Station, we think you can do this."

We weren't familiar with XPRIZE at that point. So they explained: The Shell Ocean Discovery XPRIZE is an international challenge to develop a practical system for mapping the ocean floor—all the oceans, all over the world. That sounded incredible.

At first I thought, *There's no way we can do this. To send unmanned submersible vehicles more than two miles under the ocean surface to map the ocean floor is really a difficult challenge.* But the Microsoft engineers kept prodding us, and on reflection, we decided to listen and learn.

The motivation for most of the organizations registering for the challenge would be a share of the $7 million prize purse for the winning teams. The engineers, including J. D. Marymee, Steven Guggenheimer, and technical fellow John Shewchuck, told us Microsoft wasn't interested in the money, but they would like to partner with us and, once again, bring their engineering expertise and computing power into the equation.

The Ocean Discovery website describes XPRIZE as "a global competition challenging teams to advance deep sea technologies for autonomous, fast, high-resolution ocean exploration."[46] More than eighty teams would enter the competition, but the qualification and testing process would whittle them down to the final few. It would be a fiercely fought contest until the winning teams were finally announced.

"The success of this prize," the organizers told us, "will allow oceanographic researchers to explore and map the ocean floor." In addition to the prize money for the top XPRIZE winners, the National Oceanic and Atmospheric Administration (NOAA) offered a $1 million Bonus Prize for teams that developed new technologies for detecting the source of chemical or biological signals in deep water.

The rules of the competition required that all autonomous underwater vehicles (AUVs) be launched either from shore or by air, with restricted human intervention. Then each team would have a limited period to explore the designated undersea area, with the first test round at a depth of two thousand meters (about one and a quarter miles) and the second at four thousand meters (about two and a half miles). Hearing the judges outline all these requirements, I remembered what my friends at Microsoft had said when they encouraged us to get involved: "You guys do impossible things, and this is another impossible project." As we considered taking the plunge, I hoped we wouldn't be the ones to prove it really was impossible.

Microsoft needed some suitable demonstration projects for their cloud computing systems, and they thought this would be a good one. The project design our students came up with called for a plan to send an AUV to the bottom of the sea to collect a massive amount of raw data. Microsoft would provide space on their cloud platform to upload all that information. Then we would begin sharing software and guidelines for undersea mapping to schools around the world, with the gathered data contributing to a worldwide map of all the oceans of the globe.

The first part of the competition was a technical submission paper, and we had our junior and senior high school students develop the concept and write the whole thing on their own. I played with the margins of the report and added some graphics, but that's about the extent of my contribution. It was a brilliant solution and something totally unique, because these young people came at it with youthful imagination and fresh insights. The professional engineers, with their sophisticated knowledge of the scientific and technical aspects, knew all the problems and limitations they would have to overcome. They could give you ten good reasons why it would never work, but our students didn't know all that stuff, so they came up with a plan they believed would succeed. Sometimes going through a fresh young mind, unspoiled by all the reasons why a dream isn't possible, is the best way to come up with the most innovative ideas.

Our Valley Christian students came up with a design and a solution their teachers and mentors would never have considered. Part of this approach can be traced to how today's young people have grown up with *Star Wars* and all the science fiction movies, so they're naturally inclined to think about the world in terms of futuristic scientific achievements and discoveries. But they were excited by the challenge, and their learning accelerated big time.

Of course, the team had to be able to prove their plan would work, so the students did the research to show how their solution would be possible and scalable. They also had to show they could pay for it. When we put the budget together, documenting what it would cost to build the system, the total came out to $1.5 million.

Up to that point, we thought we had only a slight chance of getting to the next stage anyway. Then we discovered we had made it to the semifinal round. We were thrilled! We were the only junior high/high school team in XPRIZE history to make it past the initial round. But suddenly we faced the reality that now we had to make it happen. And we would have to find a way to cover the cost.

DOING THE IMPOSSIBLE

By that point, the deadline to get the actual experiment ready to launch was only a few months away. There's no way a school—even a large and successful one the size of Valley Christian Schools—could suddenly come up with a million and a half dollars. It wasn't even in the realm of possibility. So I called a meeting with the team to tell them they would have to throw in the towel. It was time for a graceful exit. Talk about an awkward situation. Here I was, the creative software engineer, telling his students to give up. But I hadn't gotten very far into the discussion when one of the students raised his hand. "Mr. Kim," he said, "I think we should pray."

You can imagine how I felt at that point. Despite having

witnessed many miracles where God had shown up in my own life, with my company, my business, my family, and so much more—I could tell you hundreds of stories of God's faithfulness—I hadn't yet stopped to pray. As I stood there with a group of students, facing an insurmountable obstacle, I realized that stopping to pray with the students should have been my first thought, but I was still thinking in natural human terms. So I replied, "Of course. Let's pray."

We prayed and asked God for help, and then the team agreed to get involved and do everything they knew how to see if they could raise funds for the project. They talked about how the Chief Engineer and Creator of the heavens and the earth cares for this project, and us, and how He could help us obtain the needed resources. After that, they wrote to every oceanographic institute, university, company, and maritime organization they could find. They contacted more than eighty different groups asking for help, and every one of them said no.

When the team got together to survey the results of all their efforts, I said, "Okay, let's give it one more week. There are a couple more organizations we can contact, so let's do that, and then we'll see where we stand."

So we waited. At the end of the following week I got a call from a company called Riptide Autonomous Solutions. They said they make several underwater vehicles, including one AUV (autonomous underwater vehicle) about the size of a golf bag that can operate at up to two thousand meters below the surface of the ocean. By comparison, the most common underwater vehicles that can go to those depths are the size of a semi-truck, costing between $800,000 and one million dollars, and require a dedicated crew and support vessels on the surface. But the folks at Riptide said they had an unmanned submersible that does exactly the same thing the larger vehicles can do, at the cost of around $10,000.

Their AUV can receive a signal in deep water. It will actually take the GPS coordinates and go in and self-navigate, do the mapping and data gathering, and then come back to the surface. Once the program is activated, it does not need to be physically controlled. It's fully automated. When the team later saw the submersible and watched a demonstration of what it could do, we were all totally amazed.

Our original program design called for a mother ship launched from shore to take the AUV to the competition area and deploy it autonomously. The surface ship we designed our experiment around is called a Wave Adaptive Modular Vessel (WAM-V). There's only one maker, based in San Francisco, and that vessel costs between $300,000 and $500,000. We went to their headquarters and told them what we were doing. They said they loved our project, but they're a start-up company. All their products are made to order, and they couldn't afford to cut the cost for us. We would have to work with somebody who already had a WAM-V, because they didn't have any extras.

Well, later that same afternoon we got a call from the director of the maritime research program at Florida Atlantic University (FAU) who said they had heard about our request. He told us they had two WAM-Vs, and they would be glad to lend us one of them when it came time to test our vehicles in the open ocean. And they said they would supply a qualified technician to help us deploy the vehicle for our test.

Just like the others who had agreed to help us, they appreciated our educational objectives. When the students began reaching out to various organizations for help, they explained that our goal was not merely to win the competition but to create a platform that could help educate young people and inspire a passion for science education, such as the AMSE and STEM programs, in students around the world. The companies and the university that decided to work with us wanted to help because they identified with our goals. They said they believed in what we were doing.

That was a miracle, but not the only one. A few days later, when I was on the phone with the engineers at Riptide, trying to negotiate the cost of the submersible AUV, they said, "It's ten thousand dollars for the base unit and more for the larger vehicles, but we've decided to just give it to you." They said they were going to ship a unit to the school, and we could keep it. I couldn't believe my ears.

We have an executive meeting at VCS every Tuesday morning, and each week I report on the status of what's happening in these programs. At the beginning of the year I had told the members we were working on the XPRIZE undersea mapping project, but we discovered the cost would be at least $1.5 million. So I said there was absolutely no way we would ever get there. After receiving the phone calls from FAU and Riptide, I went to the Tuesday meeting and announced, "We just acquired $1.5 million worth of equipment." I saw the shock on the faces of some of our people. But, believe me, there was a lot of praising God going on as well.

What's interesting about all this is that we've been able to involve the whole school. The media department has been involved, with students filming the whole project. The head of the Valley Conservatory of the Arts, Troy Gunter, came to me and said he would commission Yuma Sung, an accomplished composer and Valley Christian alumnus, to compose a musical score for *Ocean Quest*, the documentary about the VCS team's XPRIZE competition journey. "Then," Troy said, "we'll have the VCHS symphonic orchestra perform the composition as the world premiere at the school's Christmas concert in December 2017."

After that, I talked to some of the students in the athletics department to get them involved so they could help us with logistics and piloting the vehicles during the test, learning how to manage and manipulate the very specialized equipment. Soon, representatives of the whole school were involved! And it wasn't just a bunch of isolated geeks (a proficient digital technology enthusiast). Like the ISS experiments, the Ocean Discovery challenge was a multi-disciplinary project. We were able to put a high-depth camera on board the AUVs and take high-resolution photos of what was happening on the ocean floor, so we'd have both a visual and a digital record of the experiment. All the data we gathered could be uploaded to the Microsoft Azure cloud computing platform, and we would then have access to a set of services to help us organize and analyze the data.

Expanding the Opportunities

Throughout this project, our ultimate goal has been not only to upload and analyze our data, but to develop underwater ocean research systems to inspire students' imaginations and their passion for learning. Students in schools around the world can actually deploy these same tools. Just think how great it is for junior high and high school teens to be able to discover and explore the oceans of the world. The efforts will make a tremendous contribution to ocean science and provide opportunities for schoolchildren everywhere to gain access to the mysteries of the oceans.

Our Riptide AUV has underwater cameras, and our newly acquired video rover is able to roam the ocean floor. So now we have a huge platform for students to study the depths of the ocean on their iPads and classroom computers. Our students are proving that this concept and this technology can explore the oceans of the world in a revolutionary but cost-effective manner, well within reach of ordinary school budgets. We want to show educators in schools all across America and beyond how their students can do the same kinds of experiments.

When the Monterey Bay Aquarium Research Institute found out what our students were doing, they were so impressed they invited our team to be part of their underwater research program, called the

Monterey Accelerated Research System (MARS). MARS operates 891 meters (2,923 feet) below the sea surface and about twenty-five kilometers west-northwest of Monterey, California. They actually gave us one of only eight nodes into their research facility, so we are the only high school in the world with a permanent science experiment platform under the ocean. Our monitors are plugged in on the floor of the Pacific Ocean, and we have students and faculty around the world continuously conducting science experiments and exploring the ocean depths.

The Quest for Space ISS program and the Quest for Oceans research program are our two initial projects at the Quest Institute. That's why Cliff likes to say we're involved in scientific research "from deep space to the ocean depths." And when schoolchildren find out what's happening in the deepest oceans and in the far reaches of space, they're being exposed to the majesty and the creative works of God. They feel compelled to ask, "Who made all this?" or, "Who designed all this?" Such questions automatically start a discussion about the fundamentals of faith and the origins of the universe. And as Dr. Daugherty has pointed out, with parent permission, it's legal for volunteer mentors to have these discussions with students during after-school co-curricular programs. It's a wonderful way for Christian mentors to share the light of Jesus with children in our public schools.

Of course, the Quest Institute offers both secular and Christian versions of the curricula. The programs are fully applicable for secular public schools during the school day as well as for after-school co-curricular programs with community mentors.

JUST ADD WATER

The AMSE, Quest for Space, and Quest for Oceans programs at VCS are revolutionary, but we constantly keep our eyes open for new challenges to accelerate applied math, science, and engineering learning for our students. After we prove the value and scalability of each program, we want to offer them to students in other schools through the non-profit Quest Institute for Quality Education. And our newest initiative is a program with incredible potential for helping people in some of the world's poorest countries.

When I first came across this innovative concept, I told Dr. Daugherty and the VCS administrators, "You know how passionate I am about the ISS and Ocean Discovery programs, but I may be even more passionate about our newest program: a scalable application for hydroponics operations. Hydroponics and aeroponics are methods of growing plants without soil, using mineral nutrient solutions to feed and enrich plants, and I believe this may be a project that can change the lives of not only our students but millions of people in towns and villages around the world."

In one type of hydroponics, called the nutrient film technique, plants are suspended in a water solvent containing mineral nutrients. In another type, we can grow plants in an inert medium such as gravel or horticultural perlite. In aeroponics, plants are grown in containers without either soil or gravel, but they are regularly exposed to a nutrient mist. Growth rates for all of these methods are astounding.

The idea of introducing our students to hydroponics came from a meeting with a Christian farmer who felt called by God to work on a hydroponic system to help feed people in underdeveloped countries. I made contact with him through friends of mine, and then went out and visited him at his research farm. When I saw what he was doing, I knew I had to learn more. He has developed a hydroponic farm and has been experimenting with all sorts of plants, nutrients, and growing applications for the past six years, finding ways to perfect his system.

The thought hit me that if we automated this system through technology and brought it back to VCS as a way to teach children about horticulture, farming techniques, and food production, not only as a botany project but as part of the school's AMSE program, it could be revolutionary. But I could see even bigger purposes. If we developed this, taught our students how to do it, and then productized it, we could introduce hydroponic food growing solutions on our student's mission trips in less-developed countries. Think what this could mean to a poor village in India or Africa or South America. Our students could teach people how to create and develop their own hydroponic farms to feed their families and their entire communities. Before long, farmers would be producing so much food they could not only feed their own families but also have enough left over to run a business.

A hydroponic platform the size of the average kitchen table, an area of maybe three feet by four feet, with a water tank about three feet deep, has enough capacity to feed a large family for life. We built our first hydroponic farm at Valley Christian High School in 2018 and set up a hydroponic table farm in two of our elementary school classrooms. We have to harvest every three weeks because the plants produced in this way grow so much faster than plants grown in a traditional garden.

What's unique about what we're doing at Valley is that we like to take on seemingly impossible challenges and engage our students in partnership with talented faculty, volunteer experts, and mentors to find solutions. Then we offer the same learning opportunities to students in other schools. So with the hydroponics program, we're developing the table and other components along with a curriculum on what types of plants to grow, how to keep the system stable and productive, and how to automate the process.

We are in contact now with a Christian businessman who owns

a solar company. He is going to build a solar enclosure so the hydroponics apparatus will be self-powered. He also runs an LED light company, producing lamps that simulate sunlight. When our students and their mentors combine these elements, the plants can grow 24/7. We have the know-how to completely automate the whole system through science and technology. Drawing on the experience of our ISS engineers, we can develop a kit to assemble quickly in classrooms or anywhere. Then all the end-user has to do is add water.

After the launch and dissemination of these programs, there will be others. Cliff thinks now may be the first time innovation of this type could have happened, because he truly believes God has been holding back some aspects of the breakthroughs that are needed. Why? Because until now, there was no outlet to deliver programs like this. Scientific innovation that can transform cultures brings glory to God. But our knowledge of science and technology has to be capable of dealing with the new ideas, and then the ideas have to be delivered in the right way. Scripture says, "Train up a child in the way he should go, and when he is old he will not depart from it."[47] So we're training children, and God is using these means to bless and inspire others.

DIVINE DOWNLOADS

When I presented the idea of the hydroponics project to my millennial friends in the Bible study group, they were so jazzed they went out to visit the farm where this idea began. Now they're going every week, and one Christian guy came up to me and said, "Danny, I'm going to quit my job to do this." I told him he ought to hold off for a while. It wasn't quite to that level yet, but that's how passionate young professionals can be when they see something like this that has real life-changing and world-changing potential.

These young career-minded individuals can be very skeptical as a rule. If you hear them talking among themselves, they have little respect for your basic run-of-the-mill activities or causes. They're looking for ways to be involved that have a real and lasting impact. After I told a group of mostly millennials about the programs we were working on at Valley, one person came up and said, "What you just described is something that touches every part of what I want to do. You've got technology, a solution to hunger and poverty, as well as education and a missions program. It's a no-brainer. I want to be involved."

The Quest for Space program was our first initiative and probably the most challenging. But once that was up and operational, and being implemented by schools literally all around the world, we continued exploring other program ideas. The XPRIZE competition, our Monterey Accelerated Research System (MARS) program, and our Quest for Oceans initiative are making a huge impact. The hydroponics farming project has developed much faster, because we had guidelines and a well-tested process. I can't imagine what else God has in store for us, but I confess I've tried asking Him to slow down a little bit.

Think about how He does it, and all the modern conveniences we enjoy today: electricity, the internet, mobile phones, automobiles, airplanes, space travel. The world has been increasing in knowledge and understanding for twenty centuries since the time of Christ, yet all these modern technological marvels showed up only recently. And now God is giving us these incredible downloads of His knowledge, unlocking the secrets of the universe at a pace we can deal with if we're really listening. Knowledge has advanced much more rapidly during the last fifty years than at any time in history, and we can't wait to see what's next.

When God delays, I believe it's often because we're not asking, as was the case when we forgot to pray for $1.5 million worth of equipment for the XPRIZE. Or else we're not ready. Think of the great African American botanist, George Washington Carver, who loved science. He prayed, "Dear Mr. Creator, please tell me what the universe was made for." And, as Carver related in his speeches, God told him, ". . . Ask something more your size, little man." So then he asked, "Please, Mr. Creator, will you tell me why the peanut was made?" "That's better," God answered, "what do you want to know about the peanut?"[48] So Carver dedicated himself to the study of the peanut, and he discovered some three hundred uses for that seemingly simple little legume.[49]

I think of that story when I'm wondering what may be next. There are aspects of creation that remain mysteries to us. When we started the next generation ISS program in 2015, so many skeptics said we were crazy. They told us, "It's impossible. Don't waste your time. Don't do it." Even after we began building the program and showing how we could succeed, people were still telling us we were crazy. But those comments just spurred us on even more, because when it's impossible and can't be done, that's when God shows up.

What God really expects of us is faith. But when it comes right down to it, we often have lingering doubts when what we feel called to do seems impossible. The Bible tells us that "faith is the assurance of things hoped for, the conviction of things not seen."[50] So to be faithful, we have to persevere and trust that God has the answer.

LIFE-CHANGING PASSION

This kind of thinking played a big part in the situation we faced when our Ocean Quest team flew to Florida for the critical second stage of the Shell Ocean Discovery XPRIZE competition in November 2017. After arriving with a dozen students and adult team members, we went to sea off the coast of Fort Lauderdale to deploy our AUVs in front of the judges. But that day everything that could go wrong went wrong. Our AUV shorted and wouldn't start, and the second AUV in the water had a disabled battery. Then on the way back to shore, I learned that the WAM-V above-surface vehicle that Florida Atlantic University was testing had run aground and was also disabled. Our team worked all night to get one of the AUVs working, and, providentially, the FAU team repaired the WAM-V just in time.

Because Cliff had work to do at home, he didn't fly out to Fort Lauderdale on Sunday with the rest of us. When he arrived on Monday evening, he learned about all the terrible problems we had run into that day. Early the next morning when we got together, he told us how he had prayed that night and felt led to give a short devotional to the team in the morning. So he read from Isaiah where it says, "For I am the Lord your God, Who divided the sea whose waves roared . . . I spread out the heavens and put the earth in its place. . . . How beautiful . . . are the feet of him who brings good news, who proclaims peace and brings . . . glad tidings . . . and Who says . . . 'Your God reigns!'"[51]

After reading the passage, Dr. Daugherty challenged our team: "God's Word tells us that it is the Lord who stirs up the seas and the waves. Yesterday was a terrible day, and sometimes I think success depends on our answer to the question, 'Why are we doing this?' So let's check our motives for competing in the XPRIZE competition. Yesterday everything failed. Today, let's ask God to help us succeed so we can open doors of opportunity for students around the world to do research in the oceans and discover His great creation. Let's pray and ask the Creator of the heavens and the earth to give divine downloads so that your success today can be as huge as your failures were yesterday."

After Cliff's devotion, we prayed together that our efforts that day would glorify the Lord and bring His goodness to students and people around the world. Then we loaded the vans and headed for the ocean.

God answered our prayers, and that day every test the team ran went successfully. The XPRIZE judges were amazed. They seemed to realize something extraordinary was happening. At the end of the judging window for this demo, we had to download the mapping data from the submersible and run it through the software to make a map. With a great deal of effort and a lot of prayers, the students completed ten of the eleven requirements. Our morning prayers were answered, and the second and final day of competition was indeed as successful as the previous day had been a failure. Then in January 2018, within the allotted time frame for this round of the competition, the team successfully completed the last requirement as well.

In light of our team's success, I thought back to all the hurdles we had already cleared. The first hurdle was my own initial reaction: "No, absolutely not." I thought we were really lucky on the ISS project. We found the right solution for the Quest for Space, but I wasn't sure we could succeed at another project of this magnitude. Still, we eventually decided to get on board. Our ability to engage was due in large part to our students' ability to think outside the box. They were able to come up with a design that was truly innovative.

At one point Cliff reminded us how aeronautical engineers had "proven" that bumblebees can't possibly fly. Their bodies are simply too big, and the amount of lift their tiny wings can generate would never be enough to keep them aloft. But, fortunately, nobody told the bumblebee!

We faced another hurdle when the XPRIZE project seemed to come to a dead-end before we began because of the cost. How could we forget that it was a junior high team member who suggested we should pray when the way forward seemed impossible? Sometimes we forget the power of a simple prayer of petition. As Jesus taught, we need the faith of a child. So often, worries and barriers overwhelm us and we forget to put our concerns in God's hands, which is where we always find real answers. That's exactly what we experienced on the last day of the XPRIZE competition.

This amazing account about our Ocean Quest team's pursuit of the XPRIZE doesn't end here. Stay tuned for more of the story in the next chapter.

Part of the attraction for the things we're doing today at Valley, especially for me and others who come from the world of science and technology, is to reignite that desire to strive against the impossible. The world is wonderful and full of hope, and the students understand that. And while the adults in these programs serve as mentors for them, at the same time the students serve to reinvigorate us with their sense of anticipation, discovery, and joy. One of the things I hope comes out strongly in this book is that not only are these programs a way for people like myself to give back to the community. It's also rewarding to have the feeling that God has specifically prepared the way for each of us to do what we do, and in the process to give back.

People in other cities and other parts of the world don't have to have a Silicon Valley nearby. The Quest for Space and Quest for Oceans programs supply the challenge. The curriculum, training, and support systems offer our blueprint for the way forward. The main added requirement for our programs is an impassioned mentor or teacher who is willing to contribute time, energy, and encouragement to young student participants.

The appeal of these projects is infectious. Here's another great example: VCS recently partnered with Sally Ride Science, an organization founded in 2001 with a passion for all children to discover 21st-century solutions to age-old challenges. Now with several locations in

Southern California and other parts of the country, its main objective is to introduce STEM learning to all children but especially under-served students.

Dr. Edward Abeyta, at the University of California San Diego, is on the leadership team of the Sally Ride Science nonprofit founda-tion. So I told him about Quest for Space and Quest for Oceans and how they are invigorating our students and helping us engage young people in the public schools and the community. When he heard what is happening, his face lit up. He said, "That's exactly the sort of thing I'm searching for in our organization. We need to set up a better mentor system to help the children in our programs. Danny, we're going to engage with you, completely."

If you have that passion and desire, you too can make a difference.

I thank God for men and women like Danny who have seen the power of transformation working through their lives as they have stepped out to make a difference. My hope and prayer is that men and women in mid-career, as well as those who have retired as technologists, business leaders, public officials—or anyone else who wants to use his or her knowledge and skills to benefit the next gen-eration—will be inspired by what's happening at the Quest Institute and decide to get involved. As we talked about all these educational innovations, Danny said, "I would have no reservation handing a copy of this book to my peers and saying, 'Read this. This is how you can use what you've learned to make an impact in the world today.' And, when they do, it will be life-changing for those they mentor and for themselves as well."

Danny is absolutely right about that. I'm not sure who gets the

greatest joy and fulfillment when the lives of our students are transformed: the mentors or their mentees.

CHAPTER 8

MAKING IT WORK:
DOING THE "IMPOSSIBLE"

WHEN DANNY KIM first joined the team at Valley Christian Schools as a mentor, he had no idea he would be part of ushering in a new era with the Quest for Space program. What began as a dream to increase the program's accessibility became a reality, creating cutting-edge technology and giving students everywhere an opportunity to shoot for the stars. But there was a learning curve, not only for the students but for the teachers and volunteers as well.

Danny and his wife, Hannah, first got involved at Valley as parents. Their son was in the ISS program, but the design, fabrication, assembly, and programming for every science project the students accomplished at that time was so advanced the program could not be offered to students younger than junior high. As an engineer with a computer science degree from Cornell University, Danny marveled at what the junior and senior high students were learning. It was obviously a great program, but more suited to upper-level students with advanced science and engineering skills. It seemed more like college or even graduate level work. Danny realized the potential of the program and decided to offer some suggestions on how the science could be made scalable for elementary through university students. What happened next was extraordinary. This is Danny's story:

When I first came on as a mentor for the junior high students in 2015, I didn't quite know what to expect. I knew I would be mentoring bright students, and their accomplishments so far had impressed me, but I had some reservations about what their commitment level might be. There was a lot of work to accomplish, and I expected much of my time would be spent motivating them to put in the immense effort necessary to make their International Space Station experiment successful.

On the first day of class, my worries were immediately erased. As I began to tell the students about the challenges they would face, they reassured me. "We're going to do this, Mr. Kim. Whatever we have to do, whatever we have to learn, whatever we need to know to get our experiment on that flight, we will do it." I loved their attitude and their determination, and in the four months it took to prepare the experiment for launch, I saw the transformative and motivational effect the program had on their learning. Their whole concept of math, science, and engineering dramatically changed. The way the students grew individually, and the way they came together as a group, was so inspiring. I thought, *This is the way education should be.*

I saw a deeper passion for learning being ignited in these students, and I knew how inspirational this model would be for those who aren't performing well or who have lost interest in school. That sparked an idea, so the challenge became, "How can we make this program available for more students?" At that point I went to Dr. Daugherty and told him I thought there was a way to make the ISS program scalable and accessible to a much wider range of students.

He gave me the green light to talk to some other engineers to see what they thought about trying to make the program friendlier and easier to use for younger and more challenged students, and they all said, "No, it's not possible." After that, Cliff and I sat down with several of the VCS staff members and began to brainstorm ways to design a more user-friendly platform, but we soon discovered the technology we needed didn't exist. At least, not yet.

Cliff asked, "What will it take to discover a way forward?" I did some quick calculations and "guesstimated" we needed about $125,000 for the engineering work. Cliff said we had enough in the Quest Institute account for research and development (R&D), funds we had earned by helping other high schools put their experiments on the ISS. So he called the Quest Institute board together and we pitched the idea. They committed the $125,000—and it scared me a bit. After the board meeting ended and the euphoria dropped, I realized we had just agreed to deliver a low-cost, scalable, accessible model for ISS research projects to multiple levels of students for $125,000. What was I thinking?

But then Cliff posed another question. "What do you think it will cost to take this project to completion?" I made another guesstimate and said, "Maybe $2.5 million in programming." Cliff looked stunned, and asked, "Where's that money coming from, Danny? You must have a plan in mind, right?" I assured Cliff the $125,000 would provide enough programming to give a good start, and I said I would call some of my programming friends for help. "This is such a transformational program," I told him, "it will inspire them to contribute their time. That's how we'll do it." I knew it was a bold promise, but I felt reasonably certain we could actually do it.

Several weeks later I was having coffee with a friend who had just moved from one department to another at Microsoft in Seattle, and I asked him what his new position involved. He laughed and said,

"We take on impossible projects. We're supposed to team up with companies who need technology that doesn't exist, to fix problems that don't currently have solutions." That caught my attention, so I asked him to tell me more.

"They call us the SWAT Team," he said. "We only get involved in projects that are hard to do, or next to impossible, and we find ways to solve those problems and make them work. The goal is to use Microsoft's Azure cloud technology, with access to some really advanced data analysis and research tools. Then when we come up with solutions to these problems, we're able to show our Microsoft partners the advantages of working with the cloud."

I could hardly believe what I was hearing. I thought, *Wow, this is exactly what we've been praying for.* So I said, "Have I got a project for you." I told my friend all about the ISS program, our amazing students, and our desire to make the program available to even more young students, in both public and private schools.

He responded, "Are you kidding? I love it." Instantly he was on board. He took the idea to his colleagues at Microsoft, and a process that normally takes months to gain approval got cemented into a partnership within a few weeks. Before long, we flew a group of our junior high students to the Microsoft headquarters in Seattle to meet with their engineers who had a commitment to solve, together with our students and engineers, an impossible problem.

At the end of a two-day collaborative whiteboard session, we had a go-forward solution. As we were wrapping up, my friend came over to me. He said, "I've been at Microsoft for a long time, Danny, and this is the most fun I've ever had."

ALL THINGS ARE POSSIBLE

Much to our surprise, Microsoft assigned seven of their full-time engineers to work with us on the project for five months. On our end, we set up a classroom of seventh- and eighth-graders as a makeshift R&D laboratory. Together we embarked on a mission to create an easy-to-use, sharable platform that would be "plug and play," using Lego's Mindstorms software and other technology that would allow students of all different ages and educational backgrounds to place their experiments into space on the ISS.

That's how we developed the NexGen ISS program. On October 17, 2016, we realized our dream: The next-generation platform was launched aboard the Orbital ATK's Cygnus spacecraft to the International Space Station. We have a video showing the metal logos of the Quest Institute, Microsoft, and Valley Christian Schools floating around weightlessly inside our NextGen experiment cube on the ISS.

We got that project working on the first try, and we were able to see live video from the experiment running on Lego Mindstorms, proving our "plug and play" model would serve as the perfect application for this project. When word reached NASA headquarters about what we were doing, a leading scientist at NASA's Ames Research Center flew out to San Jose to see our operation. He was clearly impressed to see junior high and high school kids doing some things experienced scientists would find challenging.

The first project VCS students had designed in 2010–2011 required the astronauts' involvement with the experiments. We knew that was a lot to expect, so that's one of the main changes we made. The way it works now, the astronauts on board the spacecraft don't have to be involved. Everything happens in the black box. The astronauts just plug it in, and it runs.

Flying anything up to the ISS physically can cost anywhere from $20,000 to $100,000 and much more, depending on the size. So what we've done is create a platform, now residing on the ISS, which can be used in combination with all types of experiments with a mere software upload. For the students, it's the same experience as launching their science experiment into space with a CubeLab on a rocket. They start with a hypothesis, build the ground unit, go through all the science and engineering, and then run their experiment successfully on the ground. At that point they can upload the software to the ISS and get their data results back on their computers within a week or less.

NASA promotes and creates mechanisms for schools to place experiments on the ISS, and what impressed NASA about these experiments was that they can be maintained and monitored successfully by the students. The students very much appreciate this opportunity for the advancement of their education.

RISING TO THE CHALLENGE

With a workable platform, our desire to share the technology with other schools grew stronger than ever. We got our first opportunity with the Firehouse program at Andrew Hill High School, located near Hellyer Elementary in the valley below our Skyway campus.

Some of the public schools in our area had struggled with chronic drug and violence problems for many years, and Andrew Hill was one of them. Rival gangs presented a big problem in that neighborhood, and almost every weekend vandals spray-painted graffiti on the outside of the buildings or broke classroom windows. Police officers were constantly on campus.

Principal Bettina Lopez had described the problems she faced after a Junior University meeting in Cliff's office. The challenges were huge and seemingly insurmountable. Just two weeks before graduation, Bettina explained with a sadness in her voice, "It's really difficult for our students and teachers. We've had two fatal gang shootings during the past two weekends. A drive-by shooter sprayed bullets through a school window, and someone set a fire on campus. And all of this is happening just as we're trying to prepare for graduation." It's challenging enough for any administrative team to prepare for high school graduation. I couldn't imagine trying to do it while dealing with gang killings, drive-by shootings, and fire on campus.

Andrew Hill High School serves some of the most socioeconomically challenged students and families in the South Bay Area. A high percentage of the students come from impoverished family situations and many speak a language other than English at home. Valley Christian Schools offered to sponsor the ISS program for students at Andrew Hill High School, but Principal Lopez explained that with all of the challenges they faced, the teachers weren't able to accept the opportunity.

Cliff and the VCS prayer intercessors started praying for the school regularly. They prayed for Andrew Hill's leadership, teachers, staff, and students. One of God's answers to prayer came when the doors at Andrew Hill High School opened to Pastor Sonny Lara and his Firehouse Community Development Corporation in September 2012. As Cliff relates in Chapter Four, the Firehouse program was launched under the leadership of Pastor Lara as a way to help students with low self-esteem and little motivation for learning. Their stated mission is "Empowering youth and their families to break the cycle of poverty and become productive members of the community."[52]

Pastor Sonny began attending the weekly Tuesday evening prayer meetings in Cliff's office. It was during a prayer meeting early in 2016—and literally during the middle of prayer—when Cliff had the idea to ask Sonny if he would consider co-sponsoring the ISS program for his Firehouse students. He quickly agreed. "These students need somebody to believe in them," he said. "They have the ability if they get the opportunity."

By March 2016 Dr. Daugherty invited Pastor Sonny and Andrew Hill's new principal, Jose Hernandez, to his office to plan how to offer the Quest Institute ISS program for the most at-risk students at Andrew Hill High School. When the Quest for Space initiative began, we had assumed only highly motivated students with A's and B's in their studies could handle the math and science involved. But we were in for a wonderful surprise.

Ten Firehouse students signed up for the ISS program that semester. And it wasn't long before we began getting complaints from some of the most academically successful students who felt they were missing out. When Cliff heard this news, he called Principal Hernandez and suggested we should admit the advanced students as well. So seven "gifted" students joined the ten students with four or more F's on their report cards. I told Cliff what I thought. "This program posed a big enough challenge before, but now we need two curriculums: one for the Firehouse students and one for the academically advanced students."

But Cliff didn't agree. He said, "Don't worry, Danny. That's the point of all of this. The Firehouse students will rise to the level of the high achievers when they have the opportunity and we assure them they can be achievers too." As it turned out, he was right.

THE CONFIDENCE TO DREAM AND SUCCEED

Now, two years into it, the Andrew Hill students have placed several experiments on the ISS, right alongside those put up by the teams at Valley and many other schools. In the most recent awards ceremony at Valley Christian High School, friends, family members, and supporters of the Andrew Hill and Firehouse ISS teams packed the room, cheering as every team member received recognition and awards for their outstanding achievements.

During the program, mentor Erich Shaffer, the lead engineer at Cisco Systems introduced in Chapter Four, told the students, "I've seen your work. You have the work ethic and engineering passion we need at Cisco. I want to tell you that Cisco Systems will hire every one of you as engineers as soon as you complete your engineering degrees." Well, you can imagine the reaction he got. Everyone was surprised and delighted by this promise and the challenge it represented for these emerging engineers. Sonny Lara and his staff of counselors had actively supported the Quest for Space program from the very first day, and they all felt greatly rewarded.

Looking back on the first day I walked into the ISS classroom at Andrew Hill, I remember the uncertainty in my mind. I didn't know what to expect. I wanted to get a reading on student attitudes and the motivation of the Firehouse students, so once everyone arrived and took their seats, I asked them why they were there. Their answers blew me away: "I want to make a difference," one young man declared. Another boy said, "I want to break out of poverty." Another: "I want to do something that challenges me." A young woman said, "I want to change my life."

Believe me, I was impressed by their attitudes. I told them, "If you come to class and make an effort, the way you just expressed, I promise you that you'll be able to launch an experiment on the ISS. And if anyone ever tells you you're not smart enough or good enough to do something, you can tell them, 'I've launched something into space on the International Space Station. I can do anything.'"

Over the next three months, I saw the same determination our Valley students displayed now developing among the Andrew Hill students with GPAs well below 1.0. The Firehouse program is normally a one-hour-long meeting after school, but for the ISS program the students stayed for three hours and longer. When they got their experiment running, they literally jumped for joy—and I did too. What they accomplished was impressive, and most people would have thought it impossible only a few months earlier.

One student from Andrew Hill stands out in my mind, a young woman whose parents didn't graduate from high school. "When I signed up to be part of the ISS program," she told me, "I was failing almost all of my classes and I didn't even know what engineering was. But now my grades are all A's and B's, and I not only know what engineering is, I love it! That's what I want to do with my life."

I was so excited to hear that. So I asked about her plans after graduation. "I'm gonna go to college," she answered without hesitation. "And I'm gonna apply to MIT. I know it won't be easy to get in, but I know now that nothing is impossible. I created an experiment on the ISS, and I believe I can get into MIT." In a few short months, that young woman went from a near high school dropout to a college-bound student who had discovered her passion.

As it turned out, the lowest performing students were able to achieve at the same levels as the highest performing students, because they caught a vision. They had been using their smarts in the wrong ways. Some of them were leading gangs. Some were entrepreneurs, but they were doing business with drugs or guns. When they learned a better way to use their skills, they jumped at the opportunity to change. They began to see where their lives could head, and they liked their new options.

PARTNERSHIP PRODUCES INSPIRATION

Danny's story gives a good illustration of where a lot of the growth for the ISS program is going to come. Between 2011 and 2016, students from Valley Christian and other schools we've supported through the Quest Institute for Quality Education launched more than one hundred separate CubeLab experiments on rockets to board the

International Space Station. After the development of the NexGen ISS research capability and curriculum, student research became completely scalable and much more affordable for tight school budgets. In 2017 we successfully tested the NexGen ISS research solution in fourteen schools. By 2018, thirty schools joined in the NexGen Quest for Space program.

Geographically, these schools are all over the place. As of this writing, we're offering this program to students in eight countries: Australia, Finland, Malaysia, Mexico, Singapore, the United Kingdom, and Vietnam. In the United States the program is in multiple schools in Northern California and Southern California, as well as schools in Colorado, Florida, Georgia, Illinois, Minnesota, New Jersey, Virginia, and Washington state. By now hundreds of student experiments have been launched into space by scores of schools and other organizations, including libraries.

Another story—equally inspiring, yet initially more down-to-earth—comes from Pastor Matthew Thompson of Trinity Lutheran Church, near the Willow Glen area of San Jose. When Pastor Matt moved to San Jose to serve as pastor at Trinity, that little church had only about forty members. Before he arrived, the church had been trying to preserve the past without knowing how to move into the future. Pastor Matt began praying about the situation, wondering what could be done.

He wanted to reach out to the community, and felt a special passion for the children at Blackford Elementary, a public school located right next door to the church. They have about six hundred students with about eighty committed teachers and staff, but like many schools, they wanted to offer more for their students than their limited school budget could afford.

Pastor Matt made an appointment to meet with Dr. Gabe Guven, the principal of Valley Christian Elementary School, which shares a campus with his church. He asked Gabe, "I wonder if there's anything the members of our church could do in concert with Valley Christian to reach the children at Blackford Elementary." Gabe told him, "You need to read Dr. Daugherty's second book." He gave Pastor Thompson a copy of *The Quest Continues*. After reading it, Pastor Matt was so moved he made an appointment to meet me for lunch, and we talked at length about the principles of Junior University and the Lighthouse Initiative.

The thought of extending a helping hand to the neighborhood school inspired Pastor Matt. He started coming to our Tuesday night prayer meetings in my office, and the next thing we knew he started a Trinity Lutheran prayer group to pray for the school. With the support of his newly mobilized prayer intercessors, he made an appointment to speak with the principal of Blackford Elementary, Corrine Frese, to discover the school's needs.

Pastor Matt explained, "You are doing such important work with the children in our neighborhood with such limited resources. Our church should have offered our support long ago." Then he simply asked Principal Frese whether there was anything Trinity could do to help. He told her he felt the community ought to be willing to come alongside and help the children in their neighborhood schools.

She expressed interest and asked if the church might bring lunch for the faculty and staff once a month. It was an opportunity for the church to take a huge step toward building a relationship of friendship and trust. The teachers were delighted and received the offer with gratitude.

Around the same time, we had a book fair at Valley Christian Elementary. We earned several boxes of books from publishers as a reward for selling so many children's books. Principal Guven and the teachers decided to donate their books to Trinity Lutheran for their project. Pastor Thompson described it as a providential gift. He and the church volunteers put nicely wrapped copies of grade-appropriate books into the individual boxes of all the teachers at Blackford Elementary, who used the books for the children in their classrooms.

It wasn't long before Pastor Matt received a nice letter of appreciation from Principal Frese, along with a list of needed support the church could help provide for their students. She encouraged Pastor Matt to select a project from the list.

THE SCHOOL NEXT DOOR

Topping Principal Frese's list, the acronym STEM immediately caught Pastor Matt's attention. His mind focused on a recent and very successful outreach program his church had offered. After joining the Ekklesia in Education, Trinity Lutheran's commitment to reach schoolchildren in the neighborhood had inspired volunteers at the church to sponsor a local ISS program. Fifteen children who lived nearby but didn't attend the church signed up for the program and attended the ISS sessions on the church campus. With coaching from Trinity members who served as mentors, the neighborhood children launched their own experiment into space.

At the end of the program, all of the students' parents and some relatives came to the church to celebrate the success of the children. During the ceremony, Pastor Matt awarded every student a Bible with a personal handwritten message on the inside cover describing the meaning of their name with a blessing.

One parent who heads the language department at a local public high school commented, "Most of my colleagues have the opinion that science and religion are incompatible. It's not true. We're right here at church putting a science experiment on the International

Space Station." Then he added, "Of all the educational experiences my daughter Catalina has had, the ISS experience has helped prepare her for high school more than any other."

Another father who is a professional engineer expressed his appreciation for the program. "It's the first time my daughter is really excited about math, science, and coding. We couldn't interest her before, and now she wants to spend time with me to learn all she can."

After such a fruitful experience, Pastor Matt knew the ISS program could offer a great opportunity to accommodate Principal Frese's number one priority on her wish list of needed support. He took his idea to the church intercessory prayer group, formed about a year earlier specifically to pray for the school. After prayer, his thoughts raced forward. Before long he posted a blog on LinkedIn titled "The School Next Door" asking for a reply from anyone who felt led to help serve as a mentor for the ISS program at Blackford.

Three great responses resulted in the plan that Pastor Matt, Danny Kim, and Jerry Merza presented to Principal Frese. She became excited about the opportunity for her students, and showed her visitors the school's STEAM (Science, Technology, Engineering, Art, and Math) room, which Blackford had received funding to develop more than a year earlier. Principal Frese explained, "We have this wonderful STEAM room with all you need to do this project, but the ISS program will be our first hands-on science project in the room."

Her gratitude was most sincere, and everyone involved wondered who felt the most joy.

A FORMIDABLE CHALLENGE

As Danny described in the previous chapter, our Valley Christian junior high and high school team participated in the semifinal trials of the Shell Ocean Discovery XPRIZE competition in November 2017. Our engineers knew the project to map the ocean floor would be more difficult than launching the ISS experiments. The International Space Station is already located as a platform in space, but our equipment underwater would be completely isolated, attempting to operate in the harshest environment imaginable, so the challenge was huge. We learned on March 9, 2018, through an official announcement that although our Ocean Quest team did an outstanding job, we didn't make it to the XPRIZE finals.

That was difficult news, but the judges gave a very complimentary assessment of our students' extraordinary efforts. In fact, they were sufficiently impressed to invite our team to compete in the XPRIZE NOAA competition finals for their $1 million Bonus Prize. For that challenge, teams must develop new technologies for detecting the source of chemical and biological signals in deep water. The winners of the NOAA prize would be determined during field testing in early 2019.

And that's not the end of the story. The encouraging part for us was that the judges selected "teams with the most promising technologies" to compete in the NOAA finals. Out of the eighty research teams that began the competition, from all around the world, Valley Christian junior high and senior high school students came up with solutions the judges found to be among the "most promising" technologies.

As of this writing, we imagine it highly unlikely that our Ocean Quest team can beat all other teams competing for the NOAA prize. But then, who would have expected junior high and high school students to make it to the prestigious NOAA finals? Who knows what can happen? It may turn out that the aeronautical engineers will have to review their bumble bee flight calculations.

PASSING ON THE PASSION

Honestly, when I stop to think about the Quest for Quality Education, it's mind boggling. But it helps to remember that the Quest for Quality Education is rooted in the QUEST for Excellence. What we've discovered is that when we become more excellent, we're actually getting in tune with God, because He is the highest standard of excellence. The more we get to know and trust God through faith in His perfect nature, the more of His loving character becomes part of us, and the more capacity we have for God to do His amazing creative works through us.

That's the QUEST for Excellence in action. For a more complete discussion with lots of personal examples about how the QUEST for Excellence became the primary influence in the development of Valley Christian Schools, you might want to read my first book, *Quest for Excellence*. Its sequel, *The Quest Continues*, describes why the QUEST for Excellence is so powerful and how the quality of Christian education first began overflowing from our hilltop campus to the surrounding public schools and beyond.

When Danny Kim read my books, he exclaimed, "Cliff, your book *Quest for Excellence* describes my professional journey for the past twenty-five years." He recognized that these ideas and principles aren't invented; they're for all time. Then he continued, "Your books create a common vocabulary to describe and understand what people who are really successful actually live by. The QUEST for Excellence journey is a common denominator for everyone and every enterprise that truly succeeds—in their personal lives, in business, in education, and even in government. Your books describe what it means to excel."

The QUEST for Excellence rests on unchanging, eternal principles that God Himself exemplifies in all of His Being. They are the same self-evident truths described in the Declaration of Independence, and they are the same truths spoken of by Socrates,

Plato, Aristotle, and, of course, Jesus Himself. The QUEST for Excellence truths are the same truths Danny Kim and his Cornell roommates pledged to follow when they started their business right out of college. They set out to discover whether their business could succeed if they consistently followed the teachings of Jesus in all of their business practices.

Bob Rubino is another example. Bob retired as chief technology officer of KLA–Tencor at age fifty-two to become part of our team. He could have simply continued with his career. But he was so passionate about what we're doing at Valley, he decided to make the Quest for Quality Education his life's work.

When we first became acquainted, Bob told me, "Cliff, I'm going to show up at your office door every day for one year and do whatever you ask me to do." He was as good as his word. He showed up every day and helped launch our beautiful Conservatory of the Arts as well as the Quest Institute for Quality Education. And those were only his first contributions. He refocused his passion for his career interests and his love of the arts toward a dedicated ministry emphasis on our Skyway campus.

At the time, there was a huge hole in our conservatory program, and I'm afraid I wasn't very helpful. Initially, I couldn't believe we needed a full-time person to manage the audio requirements for the Conservatory of the Arts. We had all these excellent teachers and staff with all kinds of expensive equipment. Couldn't somebody figure out a way to produce the sound we needed? For two or three years, I would not budget for someone to manage sound in the conservatory. But Bob Rubino had a different view, and he convinced me: Either we hire someone who knows how to produce quality sound, or we don't have a Conservatory of the Arts.

Then he declared, "I'm going to do it," and that's what he's been doing ever since. He has every system humming at top quality.

But he didn't stop with simply producing quality sound for events. Bob created a professional studio for students to record their music to audition for all sorts of opportunities, including university admissions.

Bob is an example of a man who didn't want his legacy to end when he is no longer around. He wanted to pass on his passion to the next generation, and he's doing that every day.

And that brings us to a remarkable story about a personal challenge that tested the commitment of Danny Kim and his two partners just as their cyber security firm was about to take the biggest and potentially most rewarding step they could imagine. It's an amazing story, as Danny tells it here in his own words.

DANNY'S WALMART STORY

When my partners and I decided to start a software company, we began with the objective of running the business on Christian principles. At the time, I don't think we really knew what that meant, but that was our mindset because that's what the Bible says. If you follow biblical guidelines and principles, we reasoned, you're going to be excellent, because that's the character of God and who He is. This was the premise we set out to prove, and the first big test was a whopper.

My two roommates and I had all become Christians at Cornell University, and when we decided to form a new software company, we wanted to try out our new belief that doing business God's way is the best way. But principles mean nothing until you're tested, and until you discover how you respond under pressure. We've seen so many companies over the years that say they're following Christian moral guidelines, but when things go sideways and they find themselves under extreme pressure, suddenly the guidelines no longer seem to apply.

We started the business in 1990 and landed our first major account about four years later: Walmart. Wow! Walmart was going to be our first big customer, and we were so excited when they called. They said, "We like your security products. We would like you to make some modifications to the software so we can lock down and secure all our stores."

Absolutely, we replied. No hesitation. We were eager to do that. Walmart is the largest retailer on the planet, with 11,620 stores worldwide as of 2017. One hundred million people walk through their doors every week, spending a total of $36,750,000 every hour of every day, with a profit to Walmart of $34,985 per minute.[53] We were more than willing to cooperate.

We thought, *"This is it! We've hit the big time."* I was actually working for another company at the time, so I got started on the coding, working nights and weekends to revise our security program according to Walmart's specifications. When we finally completed everything and the software was fully functional, or so we thought, we sent the prototype to Walmart. They sent us back a very nice check. We had never seen that much money in our lives. It was going to take our little company to the next level.

To distribute the software, they arranged for us to upload it to them so it could download by satellite link to all their stores. What we didn't know, however, was that the software had a bug. So when our program was distributed simultaneously, we immediately crashed Walmart's computers. Every store computer in the Walmart chain went down just like that. Without realizing it, we had effectively put the world's largest retail chain in panic mode.

It wasn't long before we got a phone call from Walmart's legal counsel. Believe me, that's something you never want to get. They said, "We are in the process of suing you. We have stopped payment on your check, and we're going to put you out of business." I guess they thought we would probably try to deposit the check and run, and they intended to block that move. Although we didn't have much to lose at that point, our business seemed doomed.

How do you react in that type of situation? What guiding principles take over? Will you decide to fight back, to run, or to blame the company network? When my partners and I faced this crisis, we told each other, "We made the decision we were going to run the company on Christian principles, and we're going to see this through. Even if this is the last thing we do before we go out of business, we're going to do it right, keeping God's principles."

So we gave Walmart's lawyers a straightforward response. "We're really sorry this happened. Obviously there's a flaw in the software, but we're honorable men and we want to fix it. We acknowledge what we've done, but we want to correct this mistake. We will give your money back, but not only that, we will pay for the software redistribution to all your stores, and we will fix it."

Suddenly there was silence on the other end of the line. The lawyer paused. I'm sure he didn't anticipate we would own up to our mistake, so he was taken aback. After a long lull, he said, "That's not something I was expecting." Then he said, "We'll give you twenty-four hours to see if you can fix it. Then we'll see what happens, and we'll take other measures based on what you come up with."

STICKING WITH YOUR PRINCIPLES

For a moment, at least, we were able to take a breath, but our program had 100,000 lines of complex computer code, and I was the only programmer. I didn't know where to start, but I went to my computer and began frantically looking over the code. We were still working in my parents' basement. All my test runs of the code couldn't recreate the error. Trying to find a bug you can't recreate in 100,000 lines of code would be like trying to find a needle in a haystack the size of a football stadium. We had just twenty-four hours to correct the problem, but after twenty-two hours I was totally exhausted and still hadn't found it.

At that point, one of my business partners came over to me, laid his hand on my shoulder, and said, "Danny, it's time to pray." I was seated at the computer, utterly burned out, and my partners came over and prayed. I couldn't begin to tell you what they said, but as they were praying I could see the code in my mind's eye. I wondered if God might be pointing me to one section of code. I looked at that section and immediately saw in one line how I had mistyped one character. Instead of an ampersand (&), I had typed an asterisk (*). In C++ programming, that's a pointer redirection. I immediately knew this was the mistake that had caused the program to crash.

I corrected my typing error, replacing the asterisk with an ampersand, compiled the code, and it all worked. We uploaded the software to Walmart for distribution via satellite, then waited until the software installed in all the stores. Within minutes, the computers came back online and everything began working perfectly.

It was breathtaking. We realized our core belief had been tested and proved: If you stay true with God, He stays true with you. If you stick to your principles, in the long term you will be successful. But what an incredible way to learn that lesson!

Walmart has been a customer of ours since that time. They've bought everything we've ever made, and we don't talk about the fact that we're Christians. I'm sure they've figured it out on their own. They know there's something different about us because of the way we operate our company. They tell us, "We want to give you all our projects because you guys deliver the goods and do what you say."

This experience so many years ago taught us that if you're a person of integrity who honors your word, people will come to you, and you are more likely to keep and develop good customers. Integrity is an essential characteristic of the QUEST for Excellence.

CHAPTER 9

INVESTING IN THE
NEXT GENERATION

A BIG PART OF OUR Quest for Quality Education is connecting with successful people and enabling them to begin believing they can help make the difference between failure and success in the life of a child—or even an entire school. Sadly, there's a growing gap between the haves and have-nots, rooted largely in whether or not the young people in our schools are graduating with the technical capability to find employment in today's highly competitive and increasingly specialized marketplace. We will always need plumbers, electricians, carpenters, and trades people in every community. We will always need restaurant workers and service employees. But without technical skills, even these workers will fall behind. Educational literacy in this century involves much more that the traditional 3R's—"reading, 'riting, and 'rithmetic." As never before, all students need integrated technical knowledge in almost all academic areas, including applied math, science, and engineering, to avoid falling prey to 21st-century educational illiteracy.

As I mentioned earlier, many think they're unqualified to work with young people on this level. Erich Shaffer, whom I introduced as a lead Cisco engineer, thought he couldn't mentor Firehouse students unless he had a teacher present, but he was so impressed by the program he felt he had to get involved. To this day, I don't know if Erich realizes how meaningful it is for our young people to be exposed to the knowledge and insights of such a talented engineer.

In the last chapter, I told the story of how Pastor Matthew Thompson from Trinity Lutheran Church began reaching out to the children at Blackford Elementary School next door to his church. I didn't need to convince Pastor Thompson to get involved. He felt this was what God wanted him to do. He saw the need, and the members of Trinity Lutheran decided to support his efforts to connect with those children and make a difference in their lives.

Our prayer intercessors and I had been praying for God to provide a church to serve as a model for successfully reaching out to their local neighborhood school. Since there are very few Christian high schools like Valley Christian with hundreds of juniors and seniors to reach into their neighborhood public schools, we needed a church model to show how JULI could become scalable across the nation, because churches and Christians exist in sufficient numbers in almost all communities to serve almost all public schools everywhere. I imagined God might use a large church with plenty of resources and pastoral staff to give birth to such a model. My big surprise? Pastor Matt's congregation is really small, with fewer than forty members. *Wow!* I thought, *If God can use a church this small to successfully support the school next door, this model can happen anywhere.*

I got together with our legal counsel and said, "I think we need to do something to begin a movement like that. We ought to form an association of churches and related organizations that share our passion for reaching out to their neighborhood schools, and offer to help in the most practical and productive ways we can."

That was the beginning of the Ekklesia in Education program I described in Chapter Six. After doing a lot of research to locate programs that do this kind of outreach, John Cooley, our lawyer, came back and said he couldn't find any organizations of that kind in existence. I thought, *What if we were to form a non-profit organization to reach the students in our schools, becoming a reliable resource for public schools, and challenging Christians in our nation to make it happen?* It would be an association of churches, congregation by congregation, not tied to a denomination. They would simply pass a resolution saying they believe God intends to reach the children in their community. After prayerful reflection, we had our legal counsel put together the articles of incorporation and bylaws for the association of the Ekklesia in Education.

LAUNCHING A MOVEMENT

Once the idea of the Ekklesia began to take root, I wanted to know if the concept would appeal to pastors and Christian leaders. At that point I went back to see Pastor Thompson and asked him if he thought his board would take on the same challenge. He said, "Absolutely. I feel certain our members will want to sign on to something like that right away." Then I went to see Dr. John Jackson, president of William Jessup University, which is a terrific Christian college in Rocklin, California, near Sacramento. I asked Dr. Jackson if his university would want to be part of the movement, and he agreed. He thought it would provide a great outreach opportunity for the students and faculty at William Jessup.

Neighborhood Christian Schools, a non-profit corporation my wife and I founded with two preschools and about four hundred children, quickly passed a board resolution to join the Ekklesia in Education, as did the board of Valley Christian Schools. So with the support of the churches and the other organizations that joined in, we had the beginnings of a movement.

In every case, the men and women I spoke with were enthusiastic about the idea, sensing that a program of this type was God's will. We began by exploring how this sort of outreach could benefit the children in each of our communities. We wanted to do it in such a way that the program would have the impact of an association of multiple churches and organizations, operating within the authority of the free exercise clause of the First Amendment to the United States Constitution.

Among our VCS student body and faculty, we have more than 220 churches and congregations represented at last count, and just about all denominations. But only about half of our students come from Christian families. I'm convinced that the unity of Christians from so many congregations and denominations dramatically increases the appeal of Jesus and His teachings to the non-Christians at Valley Christian. About forty percent of the freshman class members—more than 420 students each year—come from families that embrace the teachings of Jesus when they enter Valley Christian High School. But about eighty percent of the senior class members profess Christian faith in anonymous senior surveys before graduation.

Churches joining with other Christian congregations in the Ekklesia receive support as they seek to bless their neighborhood schools with programs such as JULI, a proven strategy. One of my personally most rewarding and joyful statistics is that through the JULI program in our local schools where Valley Christian High School students mentor their mentees, more than one thousand children have received personalized Bibles to celebrate their newly professed faith in Jesus as their Savior.

TWO PHONE CALLS

I recently received two phone calls with exciting news.

The first came from Pastor Linda Lara, wife of Pastor Sonny from the Firehouse program. As I answered her call, my mind raced back to a couple of weeks earlier when I spoke at a wonderful Christmas dinner, provided by their church for the children and parents in their community. All children among three hundred guests received Christmas presents.

The Laras had asked me to issue an invitation to the children to participate in an ISS experience at their church. According to their plan, adults would attended church services while their children would be mentored in the ISS project and learn about Jesus during a special Sunday school program. Since I can't speak Spanish, a translator helped me describe how parents could sign up their children, from fourth grade through junior high, to learn how to put science experiments in space.

After my presentation, only a few parents raised their hands to register their children. I wondered if my spiel had been that bad, because scores of children attended the dinner. Then a ten- or eleven-year-old girl in the middle of a long row put up her hand. I made my way through the chairs to her seat.

"I have a question," she said. "How much does it cost?"

Suddenly I realized why so few parents had expressed interest in signing up their children.

"It's free," I answered with a big smile. Her eyes brightened, and her mom asked for an application.

Now, Linda's excited voice on the phone interrupted my flashback memory. "I called to tell you we have a great response from the parents signing up their children for the ISS program."

"How many?" I asked.

"Sixty," she replied. "We can't wait to get started."

Before long my phone rang again. It was Bethany Valenzuela. Now I thought back to what had happened at the beginning of the 2018–2019 school year at VCS. Although the JULI program in our local elementary schools had borne much fruit, we had much less success in our local public high schools. We prayed every week for every child to hear the truth and have a choice to follow Jesus in our public schools. I wondered how God would break through in our local high schools.

Then at a meeting where I was asked to speak about the ISS program, Bethany came up afterwards and told me, "This is an answer to prayer. I was just at Independence High School to approach the staff about how I could help, and one of the teachers asked, 'Can you help our students get the same opportunities that Valley Christian High School students have to put experiments on the International Space Station?'" Since Bethany is a pastor's wife, the teachers might have imagined she had a connection with VCS. "Then I come to this meeting and I hear all about it from Dr. Daugherty and Danny Kim."

Our prayer intercessors began supporting Bethany when we learned about her plans to speak at lunchtime rallies to share the gospel in four of our local public schools. The rallies were organized by students at the Christian clubs on each high school campus, with the support of Bethany and others.

Hundreds of students at every school attended the rallies, and I came to witness the phenomenon. When Bethany gave the invitation to stand and pray to receive Jesus as their personal Savior, about eighty percent of the students in every school gym stood. They prayed for Jesus to come into their lives, cleanse their hearts, and bring their spirits alive to serve Him as Lord. I could hardly believe my eyes. Students from the Christian club who had received Jesus as Lord the previous year met the new Christian youth in small enough groups to record all of their names for follow-up invitations to attend the weekly Christian club meetings. Each student received a booklet describing what it means to take a stand for Jesus, and a copy of the Gospel of John to begin their Bible readings. In all, about two thousand high school students stood to receive Jesus as their Lord and Savior in just four days in four local public high schools.

Just as we were thanking God in prayer during one of our Tuesday evening prayer meetings, Bethany made an announcement. "I have a list of about one hundred names of high school students who want to get baptized in their public high school pools."

My first thought: *Be careful, Bethany. Don't overreach and put your ministry in jeopardy.*

Then I remembered the stronghold that had deceived me earlier when I misunderstood the Supreme Court rulings, about not believing that God could reach the children in public schools. I held back my thoughts as I responded, "Bethany, if you need a back-up pool, you can baptize students in our Valley Christian High School pool."

Bethany was determined. "No, I think God makes it possible for students to be baptized in their own public high school pools."

She was right. The courts have ruled that under the free exercise clause of the First Amendment, students do not lose their religious freedoms at the schoolhouse gate. When the students in the Christian clubs requested permission to use their school pool, it was granted, and I attended the baptisms at Andrew Hill High School. We were even allowed to photo and video the baptisms with parent permission.

With all of that background in mind after I picked up the phone, I listened as Bethany told me, "I just received an astonishing phone call from a former principal of Overfelt High School who now works in the East Side Union High School District. I've never met him, but he said, 'We really like what you are doing for the Christian clubs in our high schools. I'm calling to tell you that we want to support the

Christian club programs before and after school with a budget.' I couldn't believe it," Bethany said. "It's a wonderful answer to prayer."

"What do you think you will do for the Christian club students with your new budget?" I asked.

Without hesitation she answered, "I want all of the Christian club students to have the Quest for Space ISS program. They will have their futures ignited with a new hope while they are learning to follow Jesus."

"Let's get Danny on the phone," I responded. "God will help make it happen. It sounds like He's already working way ahead of us."

HUNGER FOR SOMETHING MORE

Young people are hungry for something, and that makes them easy targets for unhealthy ideas and those who prey on our children. I came across a disturbing headline not long ago that said many in the younger generation have given up on Christianity and are turning to witchcraft and astrology to find meaning and purpose in their lives.

That's an alarming thought, but I would argue that our youth haven't given up on Christianity. They've given up on "churchianity." They're turned off by what they perceive as the artificial and inauthentic atmosphere in many churches. But when these young people hear and experience the powerful truth of God's Word, as Danny described earlier, they're as responsive to Christian faith as anyone at any time since Jesus walked the Earth.

Bethany describes the same truth in her own words in an email:

We started the work, and sure enough they came. Hundreds came! It was our fourth semester in fall 2018, and in that time, four east side schools had been adopted, with over 2,400 students dedicating their life to Christ. All this has proven to us that teenagers in America are not anti-God, but instead, they hunger for truth, and long for the pure love that only Jesus can offer.

The week following our last rally this semester [fall 2018], the Holy Spirit softly whispered, "I want to baptize them." Baptize unchurched kids? How cool would it be to use public school swimming pools to baptize students? Wait, is this even allowed? In fact, it's unheard of. We know when the Holy Spirit is on a mission that nothing and nobody can stop Him. We were reminded of Jesus' final command commissioning all His followers to go out to the nations and make disciples, and He did not want us to just stop there in preaching, rallying students, and teaching them to obey. Jesus said, "Baptize them in the name of the Father, and of the Son, and of the Holy Spirit . . . and surely I am with you always, to the very end of the age" [Matthew 28:19–20, NIV]. We obeyed, and several student leaders, who were the first to say yes to Jesus, told us, "If Jesus got baptized, and if Jesus commanded me to be baptized, then I will do it." We didn't have to go down to the lake or bring them to the church: God opened the door for us to baptize them right there in the greatest mission field of America—their high school! Give love a chance. Give hope a chance. Give our youth a chance. Hope for High Schools is needed across this nation.[54]

Give hope a chance, indeed. A few weeks before Christmas, Bethany asked one of the school principals, "What more can we do to serve you and your high school?"

The response came, "It would be great if you could help bring in a Christmas tree for the school."

Bethany answered, "We'll get the tree, and we'll decorate it and the whole student center. Is it okay to call it a hope tree?"

It was a nearly twenty-foot tree. The students decorated it. Christians and people of good will donated funds for the tree as well as one hundred gifts for the needy siblings of the high school students whose families couldn't afford gifts. But it didn't stop with just one school. Three more high schools where Bethany helps lead Christian clubs also received hope trees with one hundred gifts under their branches.

Yes, it is true. Everyone needs hope. I've never talked to a young person or anyone else, no matter what their religious background may be, who will refuse an offer of prayer in the midst of a serious crisis. If they have a desperate problem, they welcome prayer. It doesn't matter if the person is an agnostic, a secular humanist, or an atheist. In times of peril and great danger, even atheists will rarely refuse an offer of prayer. Almost without exception, they'll be happy for a believer to pray, because deeply embedded in the heart of every person is the thought that there might be something they're missing, something powerful. And just in case, they want to cover their bases. For at least a short period, they have a heart that longs for faith, hope, and love.

The French philosopher Blaise Pascal made a memorable remark paraphrased this way in English: "There is an infinite abyss in the human heart that only God can fill."[55]

The foundational truths present in the Declaration of Independence had the power to break the reprehensible stronghold of slavery in our nation nearly a century later and offered the inspiring language of equality to civil rights leaders such as Martin Luther King Jr. in the 1960s. Never in all of history before America's founding was any nation "conceived in liberty," as Lincoln famously described America in his Gettysburg Address. The founding document was intended to uphold those ideals and sustain a nation of opportunity and freedom. Those values were inspired by the Christian faith, which gave the new nation legs to stand on.

It's encouraging to know that many young people, particularly in the millennial and younger generations, seem to recognize how we've lost something as a nation. They're searching for better answers, so they're experimenting. They're looking for something real that has substance. As my friend Rob Valiton reminded me recently, "Millennials appear to be more interested in the experience, and they want to make it real." That's a much better place to begin than the desire to acquire a bigger house or a faster car or some other shiny thing as a strategy to obtain happiness.

"Unfortunately," Rob continued, "they're taking on the world without a strong moral framework, and they're skeptical of traditional solutions. They want something real and reproducible, and they need someone to share the deeper values with them, but they're not getting it. They need something to believe in, and the good news is they're looking."

THE AUTHORITY
OF THE DECLARATION

Allow me to illustrate the power and the moral authority of the preamble to the Declaration of Independence, which records our Common Virtues. Its power is evident by comparing three milestone messages: President Abraham Lincoln's Emancipation Proclamation, the "I Have a Dream" speech Martin Luther King Jr. gave at the March on Washington on August 28, 1963, and President Barack Obama's speech commemorating the fiftieth anniversary of the March on Washington at the "Let Freedom Ring" ceremony in 2013.

President Lincoln proclaimed freedom to slaves in the Confederate states when he signed the Emancipation Proclamation on January 1, 1863. There's no doubt Lincoln's proclamation emanated from his firm belief in the power and self-evident truths of the Declaration of Independence. He affirmed that belief unequivocally with his own words in Independence Hall on February 22, 1861, when he said, "I have never had a feeling politically that did not spring from the sentiments embodied in the Declaration of Independence."

He added, "I have often inquired of myself, what great principle or idea it was that kept this Confederacy so long together. It was not the mere matter of the separation of the Colonies from the motherland; but that sentiment in the Declaration of Independence which gave liberty, not alone to the people of this country, but, I hope, to the world, for all future time. It was that which gave promise that in due time the weight would be lifted from the shoulders of all men. This is a sentiment embodied in the Declaration of Independence."[56]

It was the promise and moral authority of the Declaration of Independence that kept Martin Luther King's dream for the civil liberation of black individuals alive. And it was King's dream that sent him and a quarter of a million other Americans to the Lincoln Memorial on August 28, 1963, where he gave his momentous "I Have a Dream" speech. He quoted the preamble to the Declaration of Independence, as President Obama would five decades later. Both men recognized how the right of Americans to make claims for equality and justice rests on the strength and moral authority of the "self-evident truths" and the "unalienable rights," including "life, liberty, and the pursuit of happiness," found in the Declaration. The authority and power of the Declaration, which affords the promise of equal civil rights for all, emanates ultimately from a "firm reliance on the protection of divine Providence," as stated in its final sentence.

Martin Luther King Jr. announced, "In a sense we've come to our nation's capital to cash a check. When the architects of our Republic wrote the magnificent words of the Constitution and the Declaration of Independence, they were signing a promissory note to which every American was to fall heir. This note was a promise that all men—yes, black men as well as white men—would be guaranteed the unalienable right to life, liberty, and the pursuit of happiness."

In his eloquent speech, Dr. King describes his seven dreams, beginning each with the words "I have a dream." He prefaced his first "dream" by declaring, "I say to you today, my friends . . . even though we face the difficulties of today and tomorrow, I still have a dream. It is a dream deeply rooted in the American dream. I have a dream that one day this nation will rise up, live out the true meaning of its creed: 'We hold these truths to be self-evident, that all men are created equal.'"[57]

On August 28, 2013, President Barack Obama acknowledged the "magnitude of . . . progress" that occurred in the fifty years following Dr. King's "I Have a Dream" speech. He affirmed his belief in the same truths and the power of the moral authority of the Declaration when he said, "Five decades ago today, Americans came to this honored place to lay claim to a promise made at our founding. 'We hold these truths to be self-evident, that all men are created equal, that they are endowed by their Creator with certain unalienable rights, that among these are life, liberty, and the pursuit of happiness.'

"In 1963," Obama went on, "almost 200 years after those words were set to paper, a full century after a great war was fought and emancipation proclaimed, that promise, those truths remained unmet. And so they came by the thousands, from every corner of our country—men and women, young and old, blacks who longed for freedom and whites who could no longer accept freedom for themselves while witnessing the subjugation of others. Across the land, congregations sent them off with food and with prayer. In the middle of the night, entire blocks of Harlem came out to wish them well."

Then President Obama reflected on the advances made since Martin Luther King's speech and the need for continued progress in the future: "To dismiss the magnitude of this progress, to suggest, as some sometimes do, that little has changed—that dishonors the courage and the sacrifice of those who paid the price to march in those years. . . . Their victory was great. But we would dishonor those heroes as well to suggest that the work of this nation is somehow complete. The arc of the moral universe may bend towards justice, but it doesn't bend on its own. To secure the gains this country has made requires constant vigilance, not complacency."[58]

PERSEVERING DESPITE OBSTACLES

The necessity of "constant vigilance" is why we must help restore in all of our schools—public, charter, and private—the teaching of the Common Virtues found in the Declaration. We shouldn't be surprised at how people don't measure up to the ideals of these truths, but our shortcomings don't give us an excuse to ignore or minimize their importance. We do so at our peril.

Some argue that our schools should deal only with academics and not with matters of virtue or character. But think of this: Children spend more time at school interacting with their teachers, coaches, and mentors than they do at home with their parents and at church with their spiritual leaders, combined.

We have many models of these ideals, but I'll share a story as an example. Leah Calderon stars in this story about how mentoring inspired her to believe in her own potential. Leah is a Valley Christian graduate whose mother couldn't afford a home during Leah's childhood. She and her mother lived with Leah's grandmother, and Leah didn't have a workspace or the help she needed to do her homework.

When Leah began first grade at a public school in the fall of 2003, she couldn't speak English. Neither could Leah's mother, Maria, but she told her daughter every day, "You must work hard and learn all you can, because a good education is your only hope for your future. We have nothing else to give you."

Leah found school confusing and at times terrifying. She couldn't understand her teacher or anyone else who spoke to her in English. Her teacher retained Leah in first grade. School was a struggle all through elementary school, but her mother's encouragement helped her to persevere.

In junior high school, some of her teachers noticed she was a hard worker, and her intelligence started becoming evident. They saw indications she might be able to do much better. A program called Breakthrough took her on as a candidate for admission to a college preparatory school with lots of mentoring support and summer courses. She asked if she could attend Valley Christian High School.

She feared she might never complete her first year at Valley, let alone graduate. But she had glowing praise for how her teachers and mentors supported her. She was so grateful that they believed in her ability to learn when she doubted herself. "They helped me and encouraged me to keep going," she said. Leah wouldn't give up, because her teachers and mentors didn't give up on her. They believed in Leah and her personal QUEST for Excellence.

Leah wanted to give back, so she became a mentor at Hellyer Elementary School where she taught music and gave vocal lessons. Because of the VCHS advanced dual credit program, the University of California admitted Leah as a junior pre-med major during her first year of college. She also took her faith with her to the university, where she began and led a well-attended Bible study and prayer groups for her fellow university students. Leah graduated with a bachelor's degree after just two years. She now tutors high school mentees and is pursuing a law degree.

Thankfully, wonderful teachers and mentors helped Leah Calderon to overcome huge obstacles and press on toward success. Millions of youth in our schools today need mentoring to inspire them toward their personal Quests for Excellence. Will you join in? It's a simple but profound idea with proven effectiveness to strengthen our schools.

CHAPTER 10

IT CAN HAPPEN ANYWHERE

THE MONTHLY PASTORS' prayer meeting was about to begin in the VCS gymnasium. Following our usual pattern, we all took turns around the small circle exchanging prayer requests and praying for each other individually.

When his turn came, Pastor John Isaacs introduced his guest. "I'd like you all to meet my friend, Abraham Philip, from Delhi, India. Abraham launched a Christian school in the slums of his city, and he's here in the U.S. to raise support for the ministry. So I think I'll begin by asking him, 'What are your prayer requests, Pastor Abraham?'"

Abraham's gentle voice radiated enthusiasm. "Please pray for the slum children in Delhi," he said, "and pray that their families will come to know Jesus. We have a school where the children are learning to read the Bible. Except for this mission school, these nearly four hundred children could never escape the poverty in the slums. We feed them one meal a day and give them school uniforms. The parents are very poor and can't afford good food and clothing for their children."

He went on: "Our school occupies three stories in a very old building on just nine hundred square feet of land. There are no chairs or tables, so the children must sit on the floor. Please pray for God's financial support to help us keep the school open. Several families have already come to know Jesus, even though most of them are from the Hindu and Muslim communities."

As we prayed for Pastor Abraham and his school, my heart was stirred. *What a contrast,* I thought, *between the poverty he has described and the beauty of our campuses in Silicon Valley.*

After the prayer meeting, I invited Abraham to come up to my office so we could get acquainted. He shared more details about his school and the difficult conditions faced each day by the people living in that part of the city. I tried to think of some way we might help, and suggested we could send textbooks, curriculum, and other learning materials that might be useful. Although the native language in that part of India is Hindi, English is common, and lessons in Abraham's school are taught in English.

At the end of our talk, Pastor Abraham and I shook hands. "Let's keep in touch," I told him. "I'd like to learn more about your school."

Just after the first of the year in January 2006, I received a follow-up phone call and recognized Abraham's soft voice on the line. "I know you are very busy," he said, "but you mentioned about some help for the school in Delhi. If you're still interested, I could meet you in your office to update you on what is happening at Grace Public School."

I agreed to meet with him, but I needed to make our situation clear. "I want to help you, Abraham, but please understand that I'm talking about practical help with materials and curriculum, not dollars. As you're probably aware, Valley Christian Schools is a non-profit corporation, and I'm not permitted to donate tuition money or the contributions we receive to other schools."

"I completely understand. Nevertheless, I would very much like to visit with you."

Discerning God's Heart

We set a time to meet, and soon we were sitting at the table in my office. I posed my first question: "What kinds of materials and curriculum would be most helpful to you, Abraham?"

"Just about anything you can send us would be more than these children have," he replied without further comment.

I could see Abraham was trying not to violate the boundaries I had set. Then, however, sensing a tug from God to help him, I began to question my own decision. I felt the urge to offer more substantial help. But I needed more information. "Can you tell me more about what the school needs? How can we help the children?"

Abraham seemed reluctant to answer, but finally he looked up. "The school will be forced to close its doors this June."

His unexpected words dropped like a bombshell. "Why?" I asked.

"Another school had a fire that killed about thirty-five children because the school had too few exits. The government is now requiring adequate safety exits for all schools. Schools that cannot comply must close at the end of this school year. Our school cannot comply because the building is surrounded by other buildings and has only one narrow front door."

"Do you have any possible solutions?"

"Yes, we have found a piece of land that would be ideal for a new school," Abraham continued. "But this is a slum area and the people have very little money. They could never afford to buy this property."

"What is the land like?" I asked as my problem-solving persona kicked in. "How far away is this land from your current location?"

"It's about a five-minute walk to this property from the current school. As you know, the land we currently have is nine hundred square feet with a building of three floors and 2,700 square feet of classroom space. The new land is 4,500 square feet and has one building with six small rooms to temporarily house all four hundred students until construction is completed on a new school building. The city of Delhi will approve the new school, but God must help us find the money. We will need eighty thousand dollars to buy the land."

I asked for more details. "In addition to the cost of the land, what else needs to be done to the buildings for your students to attend classes there?"

"After we buy the land, we can clean and paint the buildings. We would use them for classrooms until we build a new school. If we get this property, we can care for our K–6 students and keep them from going back to the streets. One day we hope to open a high school and have perhaps sixteen hundred students in grades K–12 with two school sessions a day. Because of Grace Public School," Abraham continued, "many families are becoming Christians in a place usually closed to the gospel. We are accepted by the community because we offer the only hope for these children to get an education."

I felt God confronting me with a question: *Do you care as much about the children in Delhi, India, as you care about the students at Valley Christian Schools?* Our board of directors believed God had a mission for VCS beyond our own community. In fact, our mission statement ends with the words ". . . and the world."

Suddenly the words of Jesus came to mind: ". . . to whom much is given, from him much will be required."[60] I began to suspect the boundaries I had set for Abraham, offering curriculum and supplies for the school instead of financial assistance, might have been Cliff's boundaries and not God's. The situation was dire for Grace Public School, and a realization gripped me: *Unless they get the new land, this school will no longer exist. And what good will curriculum and materials do then?*

So I asked Abraham, "Do you have any money to put toward the eighty-thousand-dollar piece of land?"

"Yes, we have a commitment for forty thousand dollars from Pastor Bill Webb. He pastors Blondy Church of God in Hohenwald, Tennessee. Pastor Webb came to visit our school in India. He told us his church will donate forty thousand dollars if God provides the other half of the money in time."

"When do you need the money?"

"By February 15," came the reply: less than six weeks away. By that point I felt a strong burden to help Abraham and his school. It seemed like God was speaking to me, loud and clear.

"Abraham, your situation is so similar to our own journey at VCS. God may be speaking to me to help you, but I'll need to learn more about your ministry by checking references. Can you give me the phone number of Pastor Bill Webb? And are there any other American leaders I can contact for more information about your ministry?"

"Yes, of course," he answered with a broad smile. "We have a California non-profit corporation called North India Christian Ministries USA, and its purpose is to support the ministry in India."

As promised, Abraham emailed an attachment with the list of board members from North India Christian Ministries, along with the names of several others who had visited Grace Public School. I made my first call to Pastor Bill Webb at Blondy Church of God in Tennessee.

"I've served as pastor here for many years," Pastor Webb began, "and during my ministry I've seen many foreign missions needs. Without a doubt, this opportunity offers more results for the dollars invested than any other ministry opportunity I've come across. I personally visited the school and was impressed by how much they're accomplishing with so few resources. That's why our little church made such a big commitment."

He went on, "We're currently in a campaign to raise money to build our own church. But we couldn't pass up this opportunity. This forty-thousand-dollar gift is by far the largest single gift our church has ever committed to giving. That's how strongly we feel about this school. Pastor Abraham is a godly man who has proven himself over many years. He can be trusted."

Pastor Webb was very convincing. I hung up the phone with the thought, *If I was looking for an excuse to get out of this burden, that phone call didn't help much. I'd better call our prayer intercessors about building a school in the slums of Delhi.*

FUNDRAISING 101

Ever since I introduced the QUEST for Excellence at Valley Christian Schools, I had emphasized how the power of this message can become real to anyone, anywhere, at any time. But here was the ultimate test: Would the QUEST for Excellence and the companion Quest for Quality Education work even on the other side of the world, for the poorest of the poor?

The following Monday at our weekly VCS intercessory prayer meeting, we sought God's direction regarding Grace Public School and its impending closure. "What would You have us do, Lord?"

Pastor Abraham shared his heart with our administrative team the following Tuesday morning, January 17, 2006. The team then asked if he would come back for more discussions a week later. By that time, I had spoken with several others on Abraham's list of board members and other individuals who had visited the school in India. Those discussions confirmed everything Abraham and Pastor Webb had told me.

As my burden for Grace Public School increased, God took me through a crash course on fundraising. I called it Fundraising 101. Through my own experience of an inescapable pull to give, I came to understand how God speaks to potential donors about giving money. I learned firsthand why people listen and respond to God's unrelenting call, as I did when He spoke to me about giving to Grace Public School. This, I realized, was how God could easily fund quality schools in any community.

Having learned my lesson, I was determined that we at Valley Christian should give any amount that might be needed to acquire the land and build a school. By February 3, 2006, after more funds came from a participating church, a shortfall of only $9,700 remained. But the money had to be sent immediately to arrive in India by February 15 to fund the escrow closing.

So on Friday, February 3, VCS wrote a check for $9,700, and I had the privilege of personally sharing the good news with Abraham. We wired the money to Delhi to complete the purchase of the land. Valley's CFO, Don Shipley, wisely took steps to ensure no money came from the our operational tuition funds or donations for educational programs. Funds designated for the Grace Public School project were secured entirely by personal contributions.

It truly is more blessed to give than to receive. But God, it seemed, was leading us to do even more for the struggling Christian school in Delhi. The property we helped purchase did not provide adequate classrooms, and the new school still had to be built. I thought we could do more, but I would need additional firsthand information before I could challenge our faculty, students, and families at VCS to help raise funds for construction.

During the process of learning what was needed for completion of the Grace Public School project, I recalled Jesus' words from the Sermon on the Mount: "Where your treasure is, there your heart will be also."[61] For many years I had suspected that verse must have been mistranslated. It seemed backward to me, because our money usually follows our interest. But I had studied the verse in the original Greek, and the translation is consistent with the most reliable ancient Greek manuscripts.

At home one evening, I read the verse again. Matthew 6:21 was one of the most challenging verses in the Bible for me. So finally I prayed, "Lord, Your Word says, 'If any of you lacks wisdom, let him ask of God, who gives to all liberally and without reproach, and it will be given to him.'[62] Please give me the wisdom to understand this verse." A couple of days later it suddenly hit me: This verse is not a teaching about why people spend their money. It's a strategy on how to shape and redirect our hearts after God's heart.

TRANSFORMED BY THE
JOY OF GIVING

Suddenly the verse made sense. If parents want to spark their children's interest in learning about investing in the stock market, opening a brokerage account in the child's name will help them learn important lessons about investments. By the same token, if we want our students to have the heart of Jesus for the poor children at Grace Public School, we should challenge them to invest their treasure in the lives of those children.

The dots began to connect. The VCS staff consistently prays for God's Holy Spirit to bring His love and spiritual life to the hearts of our students. God was answering our prayers and showing us how to use Jesus' teaching in Matthew 6:21 to transform our students' hearts to have the heart of Jesus for the children in Delhi. It dawned on me: Our students had what the children in Delhi needed, and our students needed what the children in Delhi had.

What joy would our students discover, I wondered, *if they helped build a new school in the Delhi slums? What lessons could they learn if they saw how investing their treasure led students to Christ and helped the Indian children escape poverty?*

These thoughts reminded me of a story I'd heard about Mother Teresa. On one occasion, an interviewer asked her, "Why are you visiting America when so many children are dying of poverty in the streets of Calcutta?"

"The poverty is much worse in America," Mother Teresa replied. "The poor children in India die in the arms of God. The poverty in America is a poverty of lonely and impoverished souls." How perceptive, I thought, and how very sad.

"O God," I prayed, "may our students gain such a joy of the Lord in their giving that they acquire rich souls." I longed for our students to give the boys and girls in Delhi what their parents could never afford: a quality Christian education to escape a life of poverty. I decided to challenge our students during chapel to raise money and donate funds to help build Grace Public School. But then I realized our faculty and staff needed to set the example for our students by their own giving. Valley's teachers would need to plan creative ways to lead and encourage their students, in ways appropriate to each grade level, to contribute toward building the Indian school. I challenged our students and staff to complete the construction of Grace Public School within the next four years, culminating in the Golden Jubilee Fiftieth Anniversary of Valley Christian Schools during the 2009–2010 school year.

It happened. The new Grace Public School opened on Monday, April 5, 2010, the day after Easter. How appropriate! Well over half of the funds needed to build came from Valley students and staff. Additional gifts in early 2010 purchased seven classrooms of furniture, making it possible for Grace Public School to open the new facility.

What God did to build a quality Christian school in the slums of Delhi confirmed for me how the QUEST for Excellence can happen anywhere and at any time. There is no escaping the power of the Quest when God speaks, and there can be no true Quest for Quality Education unless we listen, pray, and obey His call upon our lives.

THE REST OF THE XPRIZE STORY

Before this book concludes, we'd like to describe the exciting results of the NOAA XPRIZE finals. In Chapter Eight, Danny described the XPRIZE journey of our VCS Ocean Quest team. The NOAA $1 million Bonus Prize was offered to teams that could develop new technologies for detecting the source of chemical or biological signals in deep water. Our student XPRIZE team completed their NOAA finals competition just this past week (as of this writing), and we're pleased to report the results. Rather than retell the story, we'll let you read the action blow by blow through the email exchanges between Danny and those of us who were praying for our Valley Christian XPRIZE Ocean Quest team during the competition.

On Jan 28, 2019, at 8:30 AM, Danny Kim wrote:

> I know our prayer is powerful so I have a request. The VCS XPRIZE team is in Puerto Rico doing the final competition. Our AUVs [Autonomous Underwater Vehicles] have been nonfunctional all week, and one is broken after hitting bottom and damaging its motor housing. We just did a test this morning and got one working. We decided to go ahead and start the competition now and are about to go out. The software has never been tested. We get two tries. The first try is now, and the second try is tomorrow. Please pray for God's favor. We are one of three teams left.

On Jan 28, 2019, at 11:04 AM, Hannah Kim wrote:

OK, guys, we would love extra prayers now. We are doing the real run in about an hour. Please pray for success.

On Jan 28, 2019, at 11:10 AM, Pastor Matthew Thompson wrote:

Awesome, Hannah—thanks for the update. We'll be praying.

On Jan 28, 2019, at 12:48 PM, Kimberley Kaestner wrote:

Let's go, Danny and the XPRIZE team! We are so praying for you guys right now. May the Lord reward your hard work and tireless nights with great success. Praying now. . .

On Jan 28, 2019, at 2:57 PM, Danny Kim wrote:

We did the first of our two tries today. The AUV dived and did a run but finished after only thirty minutes. It's a software bug now, and we are in the process of debugging it. Hardware-wise, our first AUV is running perfectly. Our second may be resurrected tomorrow as we think we fixed the broken propeller housing with epoxy glue. I found out that of the three teams, we are the only one so far to even have a functioning device that can operate in the ocean. We will try again tomorrow. We keep making progress, and my initial low-bar goal of launching a functional device in competition has been accomplished. All the students got to participate and contribute. Now let's see if we can make a full run in the competition area. Still a long shot but who knows. . . . Keep praying, it's working.

January 29 was a day of continued attempts, with encouraging progress as well as heartbreaking frustrations, but above all unrelenting determination. The XPRIZE rules allowed each team two attempts to successfully search and find the underwater chemical signal. But the other two remaining teams in the finals dropped out when they were unable to launch their devices, leaving the Ocean Quest team from Valley Christian Schools as the XPRIZE sponsors' last, best hope of finding a solution to this "impossible" problem. In the end, the judges allowed Valley's team seven tries over the course of a few days. Read on for what happened next.

> **On Jan 29, 2019, at 6:58 PM, Patty Favet wrote:**
> Danny, we are praying Psalm 20 over you and the team right now.

> **On Jan 29, 2019, at 7:03 PM, Cliff Daugherty wrote:**
> Our intercessors are praying for our VCS team NOW. Lots of prayer through the day. God gave us Psalm 20. Read it for a blessing of hearing God's prayer.

> **On Jan 30, 2019, at 2:40 PM, Danny Kim wrote:**
> Again, thank you for all your prayers. We did the test today, and the AUV was shutting down after two minutes in the water. After the second time, we had to abort. On the way back in to shore, it dawned on me what I think the problem was this whole time with the first AUV and the second AUV. It was a matter of Power. Just like Psalms that Cliff quoted says, "Victorious Power of His right hand." Our batteries were depleting faster than rated, and the AUV was shutting down. We needed to change the batteries out every launch. When I got back in port, I asked XPRIZE if we can do a launch tomorrow with this new info, and they said yes. We're

replacing all of the batteries now and hope to do a full run tomorrow morning.

Another good news today: Our Ocean Quest documentary won the Impact DOCS Award of Excellence! This is a prestigious award, and many winners are former Oscar winners. Here's the email announcement:

Season: January 2019—Danny Kim (USA), *Ocean Quest XPRIZE*—Award of Excellence: Documentary Feature

Winning an Impact is something you and your entire team can be proud of! Our judges base their decisions on the quality, creativity and technical aspects of each piece. The award appropriately reflects the endless hours you and your team have spent to create your outstanding production! Congratulations on your achievement!

Make sure to check out the announcements on the Facebook page and your listing on the website. ImpactDOCSAwards.com

On Jan 31, 2019, at 3:50 PM, Joel S Torode wrote:

Wow! Amazing! You ask us to pray; we intercede on your behalf; the Holy Spirit gives the Scripture (Psalm 20), and God uses it to give you the answer to the problem. God put it all together beautifully!

On Jan 31, 2019, at 9:47 PM, Danny Kim wrote:

I need to write today down while it's fresh in mind. Thank goodness we filmed this, as I don't think anyone will believe the incredible story.

While I was driving Jon from MBARI [Monterey Bay Aquarium Research Institute] to the airport, Stephen was getting our AUV [Autonomous Underwater Vehicle] prepped for launch this morning. We thought we had the power problem solved that defeated our first attempts to successfully search for the simulated toxic chemical on the ocean floor. But when we did a test launch in the morning, our AUV powered down again and surfaced after thirty seconds. We saw that the dive operation was so taxing on the batteries, it drew the batteries down from 17v to below the critical 12v, and our program had to shut down before the whole AUV lost power. We then decided to lower the dive speed and lower our cruising speed to draw less battery, but then the AUV couldn't dive because it didn't have enough thrust.

This was the moment Stephen looked at me and said, "It's not going to work," and we had to consider scrapping it. Just like Psalm 20 describes "the saving power of His right hand," I had a download! I blurted out, "Let's just throw the AUV into the water so that it can dive." Stephen and everyone else on the boat gave me the "are you crazy" look, but I was adamant. We tried it, and it worked! I held it in my arms until the AUV motors started and then threw it into the water with my right hand. It dived and finished its test mission.

The next obstacle was, we noticed that the AUV iridium modem was not transmitting its location. Without this, it is virtually impossible to recover the AUV in the ocean. I told Stephen we were going to deploy anyway, and told the XPRIZE folks to prep the competition area and send the boat. Stephen had twenty minutes to come up with a solution. Just like "Scotty" from Star Trek, his "That's not possible, Captain" motivated him to find a solution, and he said himself he got a download from God. He found and replaced the one wire he thought was the problem. We put it back together, and the iridium modem started working just as we boarded the boat to the competition area.

When we took the AUV out of the water after the test trial, the battery was depleted from 17v to 16.3v with just five minutes of remaining runtime. At that rate of depletion, we would be able to run the AUV for only twenty to thirty minutes. The low power was the other reason we thought of scrapping the launch. We pressed forward with lots of prayer and hope. But when we turned on the AUV in the boat on our way to the competition site, the battery read 17v! It's unexplainable how we gained power back into our AUV. The restored power to 17 volts was enough to allow us to run the AUV for the final competition launch.

My wife, Hannah, told me she and others were praying for calm weather, and today was the calmest weather we've seen. I've been battling nausea every time we went out to sea. Today I was on the boat for four hours with no illness.

When we launched the AUV, our first run finished after forty minutes and didn't find the rhodamine dye, which is the simulated pollutant we were tracking, but it had erred out. We had one last possible chance to fix whatever went wrong and try again. Then almost as if to show us the way, a school of dolphins appeared and surrounded the AUV and was swimming with it until we recovered it.

We fixed the bug in the code we've never tested and had just enough time to do one more launch. I counted the launches we've tried in competition, and this would be our seventh. Like the story of Jericho where the wall came down on the seventh try, I really felt this would be our successful run. When we did our final launch, we had to set the time limit to one hour because we were running out of daylight.

The AUV finished in one hour, and we were able to determine that the AUV was successfully searching the bottom of the ocean and finished its program. If we had more time, we would have found the dye source, but the logs only show us successfully searching. Although it doesn't look like we found the source, the XPRIZE folks asked us to put the data together and write up our results, especially the fact that we now have an AUV that can search out chemicals underwater.

Win or lose, this journey has inspired not only these students but I believe will continue to inspire more students in the future. Out of thirty-two teams that entered this competition and the six that made it into the finals, we are the only team that not only launched a device but can demonstrate a true searching AUV. That was the enormous challenge of the NOAA XPRIZE competition. We thank God for your prayers and His divine downloads!

SECOND EDITION XPRIZE UPDATE

No one expected our Ocean Quest team, a group of Valley Christian junior high and high school students, to win the XPRIZE competition. Being the youngest finalists in the history of XPRIZE is accomplishment enough. But our students refused to settle for simply making history. They reached for the stars—or, more accurately, the depths of the sea.

In the summer of 2019, after three years of rigorous research and testing, along with substantial highs and unbelievable lows, the Ocean Quest team flew to Monaco for the Ocean Discovery XPRIZE Awards ceremony.

The young Ocean Quest team waited in anticipation to hear if, by some miracle, they had placed alongside the teams of experienced engineers. They held their breath as the CEO of the XPRIZE Foundation, Anousheh Ansari, took the stage.

"For the bonus prize winners, who will be receiving an award of $800,000 as the team who came closest toward achieving the NOAA bonus prize, please welcome the Ocean Quest team!"

The kids erupted into cheers. Against all odds, they won!

Danny Kim and a few members of the team went up to accept their hard-earned prize. With the microphone in one hand and the prize trophy in the other, Danny took the opportunity to exclaim, "I want to first thank God because this truly is a miracle that a junior high and high school team could get so far."

The win by the Ocean Quest team is an incredible testament to where faith in God will lead you. Just as Jesus said, "With men this is impossible, but with God all things are possible."[63]

ALL THINGS ARE POSSIBLE

IT IS A JOY TO SHARE what God is doing through the Quest Institute for Quality Education, the Ekklesia in Education, and the educational programs now underway around the world. Although we encountered huge obstacles and heartaches on our VCS journey, the joys and triumphs surpassed them all. We are especially gratified by the collegial relationships we are building with the remarkable teachers and administrators in our neighborhood public schools who serve selflessly to open eyes and opportunities for the leaders of the next generation.

In a nutshell, Danny and I propose that the extraordinary quality of education available to more than 2,750 students at Valley Christian Schools can become available to all schoolchildren. VCS does not have a corner on the market of educational excellence. Our schools, and the quality of education we deliver for our children, can be only as robust as the truths they learn and the educational opportunities they have.

We believe the door of educational opportunity can swing wide open for every student in America based on the answers to two pivotal questions:

1. Will we teach to our students the self-evident truths preserved in the Declaration as Common Virtues and restore a moral compass in our schools?

2. Will people of faith and good will, who are among the most successful business professionals in every community, commit time each week to mentor students?

I hope you'll enjoy one last vignette about the importance of mentors: Valley Christian celebrates the success of our elementary, junior high, and high school robotic teams. Regrettably, Hellyer Elementary students didn't have a robotic team. Some VCHS students thought the children at Hellyer should have a team, so they became their mentors. Within a year, the Hellyer robotic team entered competition. Coincidentally, the Valley Christian Elementary team faced a head-on contest with the Hellyer Elementary team during regional competitions, and the Hellyer team beat the Valley Christian team! That was the only time in over thirty years when I was secretly cheering inside when one of our teams lost to another school.

Our goal is to offer every reader a clear strategy to build a culture of goodness, peace, and joy in an environment of academic excellence for all children. They deserve it! The Supreme Court Judge of the heavens and earth has assessed every child's value as infinite. He has a great love and purpose for every child who enters the gates of our neighborhood schools. Life, Light, and Learning are the cornerstones for quality education, and the JULI program (Junior University and the Lighthouse Initiative) offers new hope to students.

In response to the big question on the back cover of this book, "Can America's public school students rank among the world's highest achievers?" The answer is a BIG YES! However far the educational system in our country may have strayed, there is hope and a bright future for America's children and beyond, as Christians and people of good will commit to engaging with the leaders of the next generations.

Twenty Indispensable Principles

1. **Get to Know "The Boss."** Devote yourself to knowing God at increasingly deeper levels. The more you get to know His nature, character, and works, the more He will accomplish His supernatural work through you naturally.

2. **Stay in the Book.** Feed your soul on God's written Word. Maintain a high regard for God's ability to guide and direct through the eternal principles of Scripture. Memorize passages so God can use them to speak to you at any time. I have committed to reading God's Word for at least five minutes every day. Five minutes often leads to much more time.

   When I read, I am praying for God to direct me personally through His Holy Spirit. The Word of God is alive, and He will personalize parts of Scripture that seem to shout at you, as though God is speaking to you alone. God will use His words in the Bible to guide you through an adventurous journey He uniquely created you to achieve to bring His goodness, peace, and joy to your world.

3. **Stay Tuned and Keep Talking.** Pray regularly as a spiritual discipline. Give God your full attention so He has an opportunity to speak to you about anything, including matters not already on your mind. As you develop a God-consciousness in all you do, you will find it easier to keep your ear tuned to God's voice and maintain a dialog with Him throughout the day. Listen for God to speak into your thoughts in every situation.

   Even if the answer seems obvious, He most likely has something to say, if only to confirm your thoughts. He might surprise you. These adventures with the Lord will become amazing testimonies of God's miraculous works. Be sure to share your adventures to inspire and encourage others.

4. **Get a Heart Transplant.** Allow God to transplant His thoughts, desires, and purposes into your heart. Be willing to let go of previous assumptions and practices, even those long held. In particular, do not confuse personal or cultural preferences with His timeless principles. "And I will give you a new heart with new and right desires, and I will put a new spirit in you. I will take out your stony heart of sin and give you a new, obedient heart. And I will put my Spirit in you so you will obey my laws and do whatever I command."[64]

5. **Walk in the Light.** Ask God to shine the light of His truth on any area of your heart in need of a housecleaning. Make sure all your personal, family, and business relationships are in order with God, your neighbors, and others.

6. **Get a Clue!** Understand that a God-given vision is getting a glimpse of what God wants to do through you. When God gives you a vision, He will give the faith and the means to see it happen as you follow Him.

7. **Think Big.** Expect that any vision from God is going to be bigger than any dream you could ever imagine. Depend on God's resources rather than what you have on hand or in view. If you can easily see your way clear to accomplish the vision, it is probably not a "God-sized" vision.

8. **Mission Impossible?** Don't dismiss "impossible" options. Likewise, do not assume that the opening of promising new doors means you should always walk through them. Pray and ask God to confirm His direction.

9. **Expect Confirmation.** God sometimes confirms His message through a persistent, deeper sense of "knowing," or He may speak through scripture reading or various circumstances of life. On occasion, He confirms His guidance through other people, and often through a combination of means. When you sense God is speaking, do not be afraid to ask Him for confirmation and correct understanding. Once you receive confirmation and correct understanding, move ahead in courage to obey what you have heard. When you have confidence in God's direction for a particular situation, it becomes easier to persist in prayer, faith, and action toward its accomplishment.

10. **Let God Speak for Himself.** Don't be surprised when you cannot convince others to support a God-sized project. After all, a rational person might tell you God's plans seem impossible. Ask God to speak with people who are needed for the project in ways personally meaningful to them.

11. **Pay the Price.** As God leads, be willing to sacrifice and give all toward the fulfillment of His purposes. When God wants to stretch our faith, the process is often uncomfortable, or even painful, requiring us to see and do things differently and

seemingly unnaturally. Rational people may question your sanity; after all, Noah built an ark on dry ground. Or perhaps you resonate with Moses, who was tasked with leading millions of people across the Red Sea without a single boat; or with aged Abraham and barren Sarah trying to have as many children as there are stars in the sky and grains of sand on the seashore. Trust Him to take care of your needs and your reputation in pursuit of the vision.

12. **Wait Upon the Lord.** Since only God can do His work, "wait on the Lord" to do it. You cannot force progress even if you try. Position yourself for God to act, then watch and wait expectantly for what God will do. Allow time for God to do His work in His way. Allow Him to teach you through trials and challenges. Wait, but do not give up on the vision. God often gives progressive disclosure to His vision. Frequently, the larger the vision, the longer the lead time between seeing the vision and doing the vision. The lead time allows for adequate prayer, personal spiritual growth, and planning.

    We were led to purchase the land for Valley Christian Schools ten years before God opened the door for city approvals and for construction to begin. The Skyway campus vision seemed dead and buried. But about the time I began to question whether I had misunderstood God's vision, God powerfully resurrected the project. I have discovered that God often allows all to appear lost right before He shows up and does His miraculous work. I call them "Cliff hangers." It is a reminder that He is God and He uses such challenging circumstances to grow our faith.

13. **Forget Plan B.** Insist on going forward according to God's "A Team" plans. When obstacles or setbacks arise, pray and

ask God to show you how He wants to deal with the situation. Believe that He does not want to settle for Plan B. Do not succumb to fear. God's vision is never lacking His provision. Be open to creative and unprecedented solutions.

14. **Call In the Air Force.** "Pray at all times and on every occasion."[65] The darkness is no match for God's angelic air force. Every phase of God's work at Valley Christian Schools required a breakthrough in prayer to achieve success. When circumstances, human weaknesses, and dark forces seem to block God's purposes, partner with God through prayer to call in the air force—God's angelic hosts. God assigns His angels to watch over his children, and they are at His command to help us achieve His purposes throughout our lives as we pray and seek His goodness, peace, and joy for everyone.

15. **Keep the Faith.** Do not allow obstacles to stop you or to damage your faith. Your faith will soar if you see obstacles as opportunities for God to demonstrate His miraculous power. Let Him reassure you about His desire and intention to accomplish His highest purposes in whatever way He chooses. Faith is a gift of the Holy Spirit, and God gives us the gift for each of His works. We cannot manufacture miracle-working faith. "The Spirit gives special faith."[66]

16. **Duke It Out.** Give yourself permission to wrestle with your doubts and to work through the "why" questions. Ask God to help you understand scriptural truths that apply to your situation. Ask God for the faith to make a wholehearted commitment to move forward in the face of unanswered questions like, "Where will we get the money?"

17. **Tap Great Talent.** Ask God to help you do the homework needed to discover and engage the finest talent to help move the vision forward. Ask "the Lord of the harvest to send out laborers into His harvest."[67] The initial price tag is usually higher, but quality usually improves the bottom line before long.

18. **No Secrets.** Always share the vision God gave you with everyone who will listen, regardless of their means. On more than one occasion, I have shared God's vision with people who appeared to have modest means who eventually gave tens of thousands, even millions, of dollars in response to God's leading. Be faithful to share the vision, but understand only God can lead people to give their time, talent, and treasure from their hearts.

19. **Aim for the Stars.** Aim for excellence in everything you do. Ultimately, true excellence is the nature, character, and works of God. Anything we do truly reflecting excellence requires the work of God and is by definition "supernatural." Pursuing His excellence opens the door to experiencing His supernatural works in your everyday life, naturally.

20. **Journal the Journey.** Periodically document the ways God has supernaturally worked through your life. Honor Him for His faithfulness, and allow these accounts to bring you and others into a new dimension of faith in and love for God. Later in life when you face doubts and difficulties, written testimonies of what God has accomplished through you will be a great encouragement. Recorded details of God's miraculous works will speak to you, your children, and their children, and teach others about His faithfulness.

ACKNOWLEDGMENTS

HEARTFELT APPRECIATION is offered to those who helped shape *Quest for Quality Education*. We are thankful for our talented friends who often worked tirelessly to help us this book.

Emily Annab, our first grandchild, helped edit the entire second edition.

Jim Nelson Black, Ph.D., condensed two books, many interviews, and several articles into this book. (jnblack@jnblack.com / 703-989-2000)

Peter Gloege's cover and book designs for all three books in the Quest series are masterful.

Jane Rumph edited all three of the Quest books and did the final copy-editing. She is amazing.

Pam Watson assisted with substantial editing of the book, with an eye to removing redundancy.

Finally, we offer a hearty thanks to our Valley Christian Board and prayer intercessors who supported this effort with much prayer, encouragement, and editing suggestions.

QUEST INSTITUTE FOR QUALITY EDUCATION
— BOARD MEMBERS —

MANY FACTORS influence why Quest Institute initiatives are so successful. We have some very smart, experienced, and capable people who are passionately committed to applying hands-on science in projects that really work. One of the reasons for Quest Institute's success can be attributed to the entrepreneurial and engineering expertise of Quest Institute volunteer board members. They include these professionals:

Hannah John earned her Bachelor of Engineering at Madras University, India, before accepting positions in Silicon Valley. Her experience ranges from consultant to CEO. She currently serves as Director of Strategic Accounts at Xoriant, Inc.

Robert Rubino served as Chief Technical Officer of KLA-Tencor before retiring in 2006 to work as a full-time volunteer to help found the Quest Institute for Quality Education and the Conservatory of the Arts at Valley Christian Schools. Before his role as CTO, he served as VP of Software Engineering at KLA-Tencor.

Vera Shantz was an analyst and auditor for the Pacific Gas and Electric Company, and offers professional financial and process auditing skills in addition to strong support for the Quest Institute vision.

Michael Sprauve brings over twenty years of experience to his role as president of Speck Design. His success is driven by an ability to lead teams of cross-functional nature and remain hands-on across each engineering discipline. He has acquired five patents and received several honors for the product of the year while leading engineering teams at companies like Xerox that are renowned for innovation.

Dr. Rick Watson opened his first veterinary hospital in San Jose, California, and helped develop the largest veterinary clinic and hospital system in America, with hundreds of facilities, before he retired a few years ago.

QUEST FOR EXCELLENCE FELLOWS
— CHARTER MEMBERS —

QUEST FOR EXCELLENCE FELLOWS are among the most accomplished professional men and women. Their passion for quality education and professional accomplishments in education, business, philanthropy, and science uniquely qualify them as role models for students everywhere. They generously and enthusiastically share the principles that guide their lives and careers. Quest Fellows are transforming the next generation through innovative "Excellence Brings Influence" strategies with inspiration for students and support for educators around the world.

Angela Ahrendts is Senior Vice President of Retail at Apple, Inc. She is responsible for strategy, real estate and development, and operations of Apple's physical stores, online store, and contact centers. Since joining Apple in 2014, Angela has integrated Apple's physical and digital retail businesses to create a seamless customer experience for over a billion visitors per year, with the goal of educating, inspiring, entertaining, and enriching communities. Ms. Ahrendts joined Apple from Burberry where she served as Chief Executive Officer and led the company through a period of outstanding global growth. Prior to Burberry, she was Executive Vice President at Liz Claiborne Inc. She earned a marketing and merchandising degree from Ball State University in Indiana, where she was awarded an Honorary Doctorate of Humane Letters in 2010. She was also a member of the UK's Prime Minister's Business Advisory Council from 2010 to 2015, named Honorary Dame Commander of the British Empire, and awarded a Coat of Arms in April 2014. She has spoken to Valley Christian High School business and entrepreneurial students in support of the President's Business Challenge. Angela and her husband, Greg, are the parents of a VCHS graduate.

Chi-Hua Chien is Co-Founder and Managing Partner of Goodwater Capital. Chi-Hua works closely with or serves on the board of directors of Amino, Badi, Care/of, Dosh, Monzo, Photomath, Stash, Sweatcoin, Weee!, and Zumper. Prior to co-founding Goodwater, Chi-Hua was a General

Partner at Kleiner Perkins Caufield & Byers where he invested in Chegg (CHGG), Chill (acquired by Tinder), Inspirato, Karma Science (acquired by FB), Klout (acquired by Lithium), Level Money (acquired by COF), Massdrop, Spotify (SPOT), and Twitter (TWTR). Previously, Mr. Chien was an Associate at Accel Partners, where he originated Accel's investment in Facebook (FB). Chi-Hua was an early employee or co-founder of four startups including Coremetrics (acquired by IBM), where he led the marketing and inside sales teams, served as interim CFO, and was appointed to the Office of the President.

Chi-Hua fell in love with startups at Stanford University, where he earned a B.S. in Industrial Engineering, a B.A. in Economics, an M.S. in Industrial Engineering, and an MBA. At Stanford he was named a Mayfield Fellow, President's Scholar, and Arjay Miller Scholar. He enjoys staying close to the Stanford community and co-teaches an undergraduate Technology Entrepreneurship course at the Engineering School. Chi-Hua also serves on the board of charity: water, a non-profit organization bringing clean, safe drinking water to people in developing nations. He has also served as a finalist judge for Valley Christian High School's President's Business Challenge.

 Kevin and Gayla Compton. Kevin is Founder and Partner of Radar Partners, a principal investment firm, and his wife, Gayla, actively manages the Maverick Foundation, the Comptons' own family foundation, engaged in encouraging people around the world and here at home to use their power and resources to improve their lives and others'. Her degrees and an early career in the social sciences have aided their pursuits. Their work around the world and at home is extensive. A longtime focal point for Kevin and Gayla is Opportunity International, a faith-based micro-finance group. Gayla's contributions include chairing the successful "Banking on Africa" capital campaign and traveling to various sub-Saharan countries to monitor the activity there. Together and individually, they serve on advisory, financial, corporate, and philanthropic boards, in various organizations, and have most recently taken a role on the board of the United States Olympic Committee.

Before co-founding Radar Partners, an early-stage venture capital partnership, Kevin was a General Partner for almost twenty years with Kleiner Perkins Caufield & Byers, one of Silicon Valley's most successful high technology venture capital firms. He and his partners invested in many of the most powerful and high-profile start-ups over the past thirty years, including Google, Amazon, VeriSign, Genentech, Citrix, Netscape, Intuit, Juniper Networks, DUO Systems, and Hover, Inc.

Kevin has been featured in many technology publications including *Fortune, Forbes*, and *Inc.* magazine, and has been ranked as one of the top venture capitalists in the world. The *Forbes* "Midas Touch" ranking of top investors has named Mr. Compton as one of the top private investors in the world on numerous occasions and ranked him three times in the top ten.

Kevin and Gayla are parents of two VCHS graduates and support Valley Christian Schools in many ways, from football spotting and play calling in the announcer's booth to conducting fireside chats with students in the Business and Entrepreneurial Initiative. Kevin helped found the President's Business Challenge and sponsors the annual PBC finals in his Palo Alto offices.

Pat Gelsinger has been serving as CEO of VMware since September 2012, bringing more than thirty-five years of technology and leadership experience to the helm of the company. During his tenure, Pat has more than doubled the size of VMware, whose software powers the world's complex digital infrastructure. Based on both the great business results and also the culture and social leadership of VMware, *Fortune* magazine named Mr. Gelsinger number two "Businessperson of the Year" in 2018. Previously he led EMC Information Infrastructure Products as President and Chief Operating Officer, overseeing engineering and operations for information storage, data computing, backup and recovery, RSA security, and enterprise solutions. Prior to EMC, Mr. Gelsinger was at Intel for thirty years in a fairytale career rise, where he became the company's first Chief Technology Officer and drove the creation of key industry technologies including USB and Wi-Fi. He also led Intel to be the dominant supplier of the microprocessor—playing a significant role in over thirty years of microprocessors as the architect of the original 80486 processor, leader of the multi-core transition, and creator of the cloud standard Xeon processor family and many other key products and technologies. He holds seven patents in the areas of VLSI design, computer architecture, and communications, has received a variety of industry awards, and is a well-known speaker on technology trends.

Mr. Gelsinger earned an associate's degree from Lincoln Technical Institute, a B.S. from Santa Clara University (magna cum laude), and an M.S. from Stanford University in electrical engineering. In 2008, he was named a Fellow of the IEEE and awarded an Honorary Doctorate of Letters from William Jessup University (WJU). He was a significant founding influence on the WJU Rocklin campus and served as chair of the board for several years. He has also played critical roles in establishing Transforming the Bay with Christ as well as Stadia, a national church planting organization. Pat has repeatedly spoken to students in the Business and Entrepreneurial Initiative and the President's Business Challenge at Valley Christian High School, and advises the leadership team at VCS. He and his wife, Linda, have a daughter, Elizabeth Lee, who is an amazing junior high teacher at Valley Christian Schools and a distinguished Teacher of the Year award winner.

Gary and Kathie Heidenreich are dear friends of VCS. They have "adopted" many Youth with Promise students with their support through high school and college. Gary retired from Juniper Networks in 2000 as Vice President of Operations. Before that, he served as Vice President of Systems Manufacturing at 3Com Corporation. Mr. Heidenreich is President of the Board for Silver Creek Valley Country Club.

Formerly Gary served on the board of the San Francisco Symphony, as Vice President of the San Jose Repertory Company, and as Vice President/Finance Chair of Casa de Milagros, an orphanage in Peru.

Gary serves on the Quest Institute for Quality Education board. President's Business Challenge students have benefited from Gary and Kathie's mentoring while competing to qualify for presentation of their startup business plans to venture capitalists in Palo Alto.

Henry Kaestner is a Co-Founder of Sovereign's Capital, a private equity fund. He is also the Chairman, Co-Founder, and previous CEO of Bandwidth.com, a company that together with his business partner, David Morken, he has grown from $0 to $250 million in revenue. The values of Bandwidth.

com have always been: Faith, Family, Work, and Fitness (in that order). Bandwidth.com was the fourth fastest growing privately held company in the United States from 2003 through 2007, a position it achieved without acquisition or institutional funding. Prior to co-founding Bandwidth. com, Mr. Kaestner founded Chapel Hill Brokers (a predecessor to ICAP Energy), an institutional energy derivatives broker that became the top-ranked electricity broker in the country. Henry and his wife, Kimberley, are involved in many ministry and philanthropic activities. He co-founded DurhamCares and sits on the Board of Visitors at the University of North Carolina at Chapel Hill as well as the board of directors of Praxis, an accelerator committed to helping faith-driven entrepreneurs. He also serves on the board of directors of Bandwidth, Republic Wireless, CloudFactory, ThriveFarmers, First, and RevBoss. Additionally, Henry is an elder in the Presbyterian Church of America. He lives in Los Gatos, California, with his wife and their three sons, who are students at Valley Christian Schools. Mr. Kaestner serves on the Valley Christian Schools board of directors.

 Steve Nelson is Senior Director of External Relations at Harvard Business School (HBS), with responsibilities for alumni engagement and development activities. Previously he served as Executive Director of the MBA program at HBS for twelve years, where he oversaw the delivery of programs and services to 1,800 full-time students and 140 teaching faculty, while setting the strategic direction of seven MBA program departments, including admissions, career and professional development, financial aid, student and academic services, registrar, student support services, and MBA program administration. Before that, as Executive Director of the Initiative on Social Enterprise, he led a major effort at HBS focused on the leadership, management, and governance of nonprofit organizations and the role of business in society. Mr. Nelson earned his MBA from Harvard Business School and a B.S. degree from Northwestern University in chemistry, with a concentration in biochemistry and molecular biology. He has served as Associate Director of Admissions and Associate Director of Development at HBS, and later as Director of Leadership Giving at Harvard Law School. He currently serves on the board of The Harvard Cooperative Society (The COOP) and the Council of 125 at Gordon College. He has served on the boards of the Northwestern Alumni Association and several non-profit organizations. Steve helped launch the President's Business Challenge at Valley Christian High School and has served as a finalist judge and a mentor and coach. He joined the executive team of Valley Christian Schools in January 2020 as Chief Relationship Officer.

These charter members set the bar for the quality of the QUEST for Excellence Fellows, a cohort that will continue to grow and expand worldwide. Being a QUEST for Excellence Fellow brings recognition for one's life work of giving and educating, and allows the Fellow to join a group of like-minded men and women with the common goal of transforming and inspiring the next generation of students. To see the latest list of Fellows, visit www.thequestinstitute.com/questfellows.

ENDNOTES

All websites accessed as of February 2019

Chapter 1

1. From Romans 14:17, NLT

2. Colossians 3:23, NKJV

3. Access to the omnis is fully described in my second book, *The Quest Continues*.

4. James 1:5, NKJV

Chapter 2

5. Daniel 1:4, NASB

6. Daniel 6:3, KJV

7. Daniel 5:14, NKJV

8. Genesis 1:27, NLT

9. Alexis de Tocqueville, *Democracy in America*, Volume I 1835, https://www.gutenberg.org/files/815/815-h/815-h.htm, Introductory Chapter, paragraph 23

10. https://caselaw.findlaw.com/us-supreme-court/374/203.html

11. Congressional Prayer Caucus Foundation, December 11, 2013, "The Effects of Removing Prayer and the Bible From the Schools in 1962." William Jeynes, PhD, is Professor of Education at California State University, Long Beach: https://www.cnsnews.com/news/article/penny-starr/education-expert-removing-bible-prayer-public-schools-has-caused-decline

12. Alexis de Tocqueville, *Democracy in America*, Volumes I 1835 and II 1840, Kindle, Loc 6326

13. Alexis de Tocqueville, *Democracy in America*, Volumes I 1835 and II 1840, Kindle, Loc 852

14. "Homeschooling in the United States: 2012," report by the U.S. Department of Education, April 2017. https://nces.ed.gov/pubs2016/2016096rev.pdf

Chapter 3

15. A student trip is one round trip by a student mentor between the mentor's home school and a public school mentoring assignment.

16. Proverbs 31:9, NASB

17. Matthew 19:26, Mark 10:27, NKJV

18. From Mark 9:24, NKJV; see story in Mark 9:14–29.

19. See Matthew 18:20.

20. The Quest Institute for Quality Education™ was established as a 501(c)3 non-profit corporation in 2006 to serve as a conduit of Valley Christian Schools' innovative intellectual properties to public and private schools, with a goal to advance quality education while reaffirming the legacy of America's Founding Fathers as a restored moral compass.

21. The Internet of Things (IoT) is the network of physical devices, vehicles, home appliances, and other items embedded with electronics, software, sensors, actuators, and connectivity which enables these things to connect and exchange data, creating opportunities for more direct integration of the physical world into computer-based systems, resulting in efficiency improvements, economic benefits, and reduced human exertions. See https://en.wikipedia.org/wiki/Internet_of_things.

Chapter 4

22. "The Fairey Swordfish, Albacore, & Barracuda," https://www.airvectors.net/avsword.html

23. https://www.dailymail.co.uk/news/article-1191813/Pilot-sank-Bismarck-tells-tale-70-years.html. John Moffat lived June 17, 1919–December 11, 2016.

24. Romans 8:31, NKJV

25. Winston Churchill at Harrow School, October 29, 1941. https://winstonchurchill.org/resources/speeches/1941-1945-war-leader/never-give-in/

26. OECD: PISA 2015 Results in Focus. https://www.oecd.org/pisa/pisa-2015-results-in-focus.pdf

27. Mortimer B. Zuckerman, "Why Math and Science Education Means More Jobs," *U.S. News & World Report*, September 27, 2011. https://www.usnews.com/opinion/articles/2011/09/27/why-math-and-science-education-means-more-jobs

Chapter 5

28. "Open Letter to the American People," page 1 in Mary Bruce and John Bridgeland, *The Mentoring Effect: Young People's Perspectives on the Outcomes and Availability of Mentoring*. A report for MENTOR: The National Mentoring Partnership, January 2014, by Civic Enterprises in association with Hart Research Associates. https://www.mentoring.org/new-site/wp-content/uploads/2015/09/The_Mentoring_Effect_Full_Report.pdf

29. Luke 7:9, NIV

Chapter 6

30. Tinker v. Des Moines Independent Community School District, 393 U.S. 503 (1969). The majority opinion reads in part: "It can hardly be argued that either students or teachers shed their constitutional rights to freedom of speech or expression at the schoolhouse gate." https://supreme.justia.com/cases/federal/us/393/503/case.html

31. See Matthew 14:15–16, NLT.

32. John 6:9, NKJV

33. From Matthew 14:18–21, NLT

34. See the stories in John 6:1–14 (cf. Matthew 14:14–21) and Matthew 15:32–38.

35. Matthew 5:14, NKJV, NASB, NIV, and others

36. https://www.bartleby.com/348/authors/506.html

37. https://www.goodreads.com/quotes/85597-education-is-teaching-our-children-to-desire-the-right-things

38. From George Washington to the Protestant Episcopal Church, 19 August 1789, https://founders.archives.gov/documents/Washington/05-03-02-0289

39. Ibid.

40. Ronald Reagan, Address to the First Annual Conservative Political Action Conference, Washington, DC. January 25, 1974. www.cfif.org/htdocs/freedomline/current/america/governor_ronald_reagan.htm

41. "The Role of Character Education in Public Schools," California Department of Education. https://www.cde.ca.gov/ls/yd/ce/charactered.asp. See also https://leginfo.legislature.ca.gov/faces/codes_displaySection.xhtml?sectionNum=233.5&lawCode=EDC

42. "Elementary Makes the Grade!" California Department of Education, 1999. Cited at https://www.cde.ca.gov/ls/yd/ce/

43. Character.org, https://www.character.org/more-resources/character-education-legislation. See also "Character Education—What States Are Doing," https://www.character.org/wp-content/uploads/What-States-Are-Doing.pdf.

44. Theodore Roosevelt, "Character and Success," *The Outlook*, March 31, 1900. https://www.foundationsmag.com/tr-character.html

Chapter 7

45. See Matthew 28:19–20, John 10:10b, Romans 14:17, NLT

46. Shell Ocean Discovery XPRIZE: Discovering the Mysteries of the Deep Sea. https://oceandiscovery.xprize.org

47. Proverbs 22:6, NKJV

48. David B. Calhoun, "Profile in Faith: George Washington Carver (1860–1943)," from the Summer 2013 issue of *Knowing & Doing*, C.S. Lewis Institute. https://www.cslewisinstitute.org/George_Washington_Carver_FullArticle

49. Glenn Clark, *The Man Who Talks with the Flowers: The Intimate Life Story of Dr. George Washington Carver* (United States of America: Dancing Unicorn Books, 2016), pp. 370–375

50. Hebrews 11:1, NASB

51. Isaiah 51:15–16 and 52:7, NLV

Chapter 8

52. The Firehouse Community Development Center, https://www.the-firehouse.org

53. "Walmart Company Statistics," Statistic Brain Research Institute. https://www.statisticbrain.com/walmart-company-statistics/ (sourced March 1, 2018)

Chapter 9

54. Email from Bethany Valenzuela to Cliff Daugherty, Subject: Hope for High Schools, Date: Wednesday, January 9, 2019

55. Taken from Blaise Pascal's *Pensées* (148/428)

56. Abraham Lincoln, Address in Independence Hall, Philadelphia, Pennsylvania, February 22, 1861. Source: *The Collected Works of Abraham Lincoln*, edited by Roy P. Basler et al., 1953. http://www.abrahamlincolnonline.org/lincoln/speeches/philadel.htm

57. Rev. Dr. Martin Luther King Jr., "I Have a Dream. . .," Remarks at the "March on Washington," August 28, 1963. https://www.archives.gov/files/press/exhibits/dream-speech.pdf

58. Barack Obama, "Full Transcript: President Obama's Speech on the 50th Anniversary of the March on Washington," *The Washington Post*, August 28, 2013. https://www.washingtonpost.com/politics/transcript-president-obamas-speech-on-the-50th-anniversary-of-the-march-on-washington/2013/08/28/0138e01e-0ffb-11e3-8cdd-bcdc09410972_story.html?utm_term=.5417c8693fac

59. Breakthrough Silicon Valley, https://www.breakthroughsv.org/home/

Chapter 10

60. Luke 12:48, NKJV

61. Matthew 6:21, NKJV

62. James 1:5, NKJV

63. Matthew 19:26, NKJV

The Twenty Indispensable Principles

64. Ezekiel 36:26–27, NLT

65. Ephesians 6:18, NLT

66. From 1 Corinthians 12:9, NLT

67. From Luke 10:2, NKJV